The Daily Of

Publications of the Joint Liturgical Group established in 1963

The Renewal of Worship 1965 (OUP)

The Calendar and Lectionary 1967 (OUP)

The Daily Office 1968;
10th corrected impression 1973 (SPCK and Epworth)

An Additional Lectionary 1969 (SPCK and Epworth)

Holy Week Services 1971 (SPCK and Epworth)

Initiation and Eucharist 1972 (SPCK)

Worship and the Child 1975 (SPCK)

The Daily Office Revised 1978 (SPCK)

The Joint Liturgical Group

The Daily Office Revised

With Other Prayers and Services

EDITED BY RONALD C. D. JASPER

London SPCK

First published 1978
SPCK
Holy Trinity Church
Marylebone Road
London NW1 4DU

Printed in Great Britain by
McCorquodale Printers Limited

ISBN 0 281 03636 5

CONTENTS

MEMBERS OF THE JOINT LITURGICAL GROUP

The Church of England
The Revd D. C. Gray
The Very Revd R. C. D. Jasper

The Church of Scotland
The Revd J. C. Stewart
The Revd A. Stewart Todd

The Baptist Union of Great Britain and Ireland
The Revd N. Clark
The Revd M. F. Williams

The United Reformed Church
The Revd R. A. Davies
The Revd D. McIlhagga

The Episcopal Church in Scotland
The Revd Canon A. O. Barkway

The Methodist Church
The Revd A. Raymond George
The Revd Gordon S. Wakefield

The Roman Catholic Church
The Rt Revd Mgr G. A. Tomlinson
The Revd H. E. Winstone

The Churches of Christ
The Revd Dr W. G. Baker

PREFACE

This little book has been produced in the hope that it will be of help both in private prayer and public worship. It is intended not as an alternative to official Service Books but as a supplement to them. Material has come from a variety of sources and includes a revised form of the JLG Daily Office. All members of the Group, which includes representatives of the Anglican, Roman Catholic, Methodist, Baptist, and United Reformed Churches, the Church of Scotland, and the Churches of Christ, have co-operated in compiling this volume. We are grateful to them, and to those who have provided us with material or who have given us permission to use prayers from other books.

NEVILLE CLARK *Chairman*
RONALD C. D. JASPER *Secretary*
Joint Liturgical Group

INTRODUCTORY ESSAY

INTRODUCTORY ESSAY

Like much else in the life of grace, prayer starts as a fact of nature. Animals and birds make noises when they want their food, and it ill becomes rational creatures if they snatch at the blessings and resources of the world without any acknowledgement either of a Providence greater than themselves, or of their dependence on one another. 'Give us this day our daily bread.'

Maurice Nédoncelle in *The Nature and Use of Prayer*[1] considers prayer 'as from man to man', its place in 'the domain of the vocative', before he turns to our address to God. Our requests to the 'Most High' will not be acceptable unless we learn how to speak to the lowly.

And it is not only petition which is an instinctive human activity. We experience adoration whether we have Christian faith or no. The word, from the Latin, means, literally, 'praying towards . . .', and we adore whenever we are taken out of ourselves. Human love furnishes the universal example, but listening to music, observing 'the grandeur of the starry heavens above' (even though man has now taken samples of Martian dust), watching the innings of a great batsman, or even, as with Bishop Gore on his deathbed, reading the stories of P. G. Wodehouse, may carry some minds into regions of 'ineffable glory'. Sometimes indeed our churchly idea of adoration and the language in which it is expressed may be frozen in analogies from the natural order, which are too conditioned by the forms of particular or past cultures. Some traditional prayers have conceived of God as an absolute monarch to whom we must do homage in the right way, else he will destroy us. 'Kiss the Son lest he be angry.' Teilhard de Chardin spoke well when he said that in our time the need to adore becomes 'more specific, more subtle and more magnificent.' Simply as human beings we must correct and enlarge our adoration from our awareness of the wonder and immensity of the universe.

But for Christians our instinctive prayers must be both censored and transformed because they are offered 'through Jesus Christ our Lord'. Our natural theology which is sometimes too naive,

[1]Translation published by Burns & Oates 1964.

sometimes too arrogant, sometimes too agnostic (though the gospel does not, *pace* Browning, 'answer all questions in the earth and out of it') needs to be brought into the school of Christ's Cross and Resurrection. This is why the prayers which follow are all related to Christ and to those saving events through which we begin to perceive the ways of God to man.

This is particularly true of those elements of prayer which are especially represented here—penitence, intercession, and thanksgiving. Adoration will nearly always lead to penitence, even when it is not specifically related to God, as with Lord George Hell, in Max Beerbohm's story of *The Happy Hypocrite*, who beheld the pure, unravished chorus girl and saw as in a mirror his own hideousness. The Christian is similarly overwhelmed when he 'looks to Jesus' and discerns the perfection of the divine love.

Penitence for the Christian is a perpetual state in this life. As Luther said, he is 'always a sinner, always penitent, always justified'. Sometimes penitence will be a short and simple act like the wiping of shoes at the door of a house where one is a guest:

> One does not go on talking about the mud. It is not decent.
> To carry so much as the memory and anxiety about mud
> into the temple
> And the preoccupation and thought of mud
> Is in fact to carry mud into the temple.
> . . . .
> On the threshold of my temple, on the threshold of my
> night, wipe your feet and don't let's mention it again.[1]

'He that is bathed needeth not save to wash his feet, but is clean every whit . . .'

Yet there may be need for a more detailed self-examination in response to the word of God. There is this to be said for the traditional Anglican place for the confession of sin in the Eucharist between the Ministry of the Word and the Liturgy of the Upper Room, that we cannot begin to understand our errors and their enormity, the sins that we have done and the sin that we are, until they have been exposed by the hearing of the gospel. But even so, the Christian is not to be forever like the prodigal in the pigsty.

[1] Charles Péguy, *The Mystery of the Holy Innocents*, tr. P. Pakenham (Harvill Press 1975).

The moment he says, 'I will arise and go to my Father', he is sure of his welcome home. And therefore these confessions are not overlengthy, though the supplications are detailed and searching.

Intercession is also an act of prayer which our humanity demands, but it causes great theological difficulties. I cannot but pray for those whom I love in all circumstances of their lives, and if I have the slightest spark of human feeling within me, I must bring before God the needs and sufferings of the world. But what difference does it make? It is good for me. It helps to break the narrow confines of my self-centredness, my preoccupation with the 'I, mine, me, and the like'; if I pray thoughtfully and intelligently, it increases my understanding of the human situation, though it may make me ever less certain of the answers to the problems of mankind, less dogmatic, more confused. But what effect does it have on God and through him on the world? Does it change his mind, as Abraham hoped when he interceded for Sodom? Does it become a channel whereby God's mercy may stream into the creation, and the great and inexhaustible reservoir of his love, otherwise untapped, flow into the lives of men?

Both of these last two questions throw some light on the matter. The Bible, though it does not for one moment regard God and man as equals, always shows them as persons in encounter. And it is part of man's dignity and status in creation that he is able to talk to God, to plead and argue with him, sometimes to complain. Prayer in Scripture is never a passive submission to the divine will, but an active acceptance, though sometimes with understandable reluctance; and it is never an absorption into the Infinite, always a dynamic personal relationship.

The paradox of the Bible is that God is at once so powerful and so weak. The rightful Lord of the Universe, 'whose voice commands the tempest forth and stills the stormy wave', is seen most clearly in the darkness of Calvary and the dereliction of the Crucified. Only as we enter that darkness, as we share the weakness of love, and receive some of the blows which the great wrestler for truth and righteousness takes himself in the long Good Friday of the world, are we able to be the servants of God's purpose. And, at its most intense, intercession is nothing less than a kneeling beside Christ in Gethsemane.

But intercession must always be accompanied by thanksgiving, otherwise the Christian faith would be all agony and no gospel. God has triumphed through the Cross, and though his victory will be hidden from the world until kingdom come, Christian believers see it and rejoice in it and strive to continue it.

We often neglect thanksgiving. We may be too sophisticated simply to 'count our blessings', and there is something repugnant to the Christian about giving thanks for his own good fortune when the world is in such dire distress. But thanksgiving is redeemed from complacency and self-satisfaction if we see it on the other side of the Cross. We give thanks because 'the victory remains with love'. Our joy, no more than God's, is callous and unfeeling; it is the flowering of the tree of defeat, which has become the tree of glory. The Canticles from the Old Testament are to be interpreted as proleptic of the triumph of Jesus by love alone, and they unite us with all those whose hope is in God, though the fulfilment of his promise is seen and greeted from afar.

In some of these prayers thanksgiving succeeds intercession. In what is perhaps the classic shape of the Christian liturgy it is the other way on, and our acts of remembrance, and, sometimes, of special intercession, as in the canon of the Roman Mass, are brought into as close a relationship as possible to the mystery of God's redeeming acts and are seen to derive from the love of Calvary and Easter. But the pattern of the daily devotions may also be justified evangelically.

We pray first for the world, society, personal relationships, the Church, the suffering, the sick, and the departed. Each intercession, though the language is factual and restrained, will bring us into fellowship with the Word made flesh, the incarnate life which leads to the Cross and beyond. And then we look out on the whole universe and towards its original purpose and its restoration in Christ. And we are thankful.

Christian prayer has always, as befits biblical and incarnational religion, been conscious of time. It has regarded the beginning and ending of the day as of especial solemnity and has turned aside for devotions at regular intervals in the course of the hours. It has also been sensitive to what happened on particular days and times. Sometimes it has gone back to Genesis 1 and the seven days of creation and tried with varying degrees of success to relate them to those events of the gospel, which the New Testament writers ascribe to specific times. It has done best of all with Friday, the fifth day, on which man was created (and fell, so it is somewhat dubiously inferred), and on which Christ died to undo the consequences of Adam's sin and create mankind anew.

Such typology appeals to few people today, and these prayers are mostly free of it. But Friday is kept for the commemoration of the Cross; and Thursday, following the Acts of the Apostles, concentrates on the Ascension, though, since this is so closely linked to the Resurrection and hardly distinguished from it by some of the New Testament books, Thursday's subject includes all the elements of the divine victory. There is no attempt at a near-theological progression, but the main themes are all objective, that is, they affirm what God has done, and turn our gaze towards his revelation in Christ before we go on to think of the world, to bear the cross of intercession, and to celebrate God's salvation and our hope.

Implicit in the above and in these devotions is the conclusion that Christian prayer is made complete in the Eucharist. It is therefore appropriate that an ecumenical canon should be included here. In that act of the Christian family we behold God's glory in the Cross and are united with the prayer which is at once the cry of forsakenness as God takes upon himself the agony of his creation, and the shouting of the sons of God for joy.

GORDON S. WAKEFIELD

THE EUCHARISTIC CANON

THE EUCHARISTIC CANON

Almighty God, Eternal Father,
it is our duty and delight
at all times and in all places
to give you thanks and praise.
You are the creator of all things
and the source of all life,
in whom we live and move and have our being.
You have given us your only Son, Jesus Christ,
to free us from the slavery of sin
and to make us heirs of eternal life.
He was born as one of us,
was obedient to your will,
and accepted death upon the cross:
you raised him from the dead
and have made him Lord of all.
You send us your Spirit
  to guide us into the truth,
  to bring us reconciliation and peace,
  and to renew us as the Body of your Son.

(And now we give you thanks . . .)

We praise you, for you are God.
All **We acclaim you, for you are the Lord.**
We worship you, eternal Father:
and with the whole company of heaven
we sing in endless praise:
Holy, holy, holy Lord,
God of power and might.
Heaven and earth are full of your glory.
Hosanna in the highest.

***Blessed is he who comes in the name of the Lord.**
Hosanna in the highest.

*This may be used at other appropriate points, or omitted.

Heavenly Father,
we offer you this praise
through Jesus Christ, your only Son, our Lord,
who hallowed your name,
accomplished your will,
established your kingdom,
and gave himself to be our spiritual food.
And now we pray that by the power of your Holy Spirit
these gifts of bread and wine
may be to us his body and his blood.
For on the night when he was betrayed
he took bread, and when he had given thanks,
he broke it, and said,
'Take, eat: this is my body which is for you.
Do this in remembrance of me.'
In the same way after supper, he took the cup, saying,
'This cup is the new covenant in my blood.
Do this, as often as you drink it,
in remembrance of me.'
Therefore, heavenly Father,
obeying the command of your dear Son,
and looking for his coming again in glory,
we celebrate the perfect sacrifice of his death upon the cross,
his mighty resurrection and his glorious ascension.

All **Christ is Victor.**
Christ is King.
Christ is Lord of all.

Father, accept through Christ
our sacrifice of thanks and praise:
and as we eat and drink these holy gifts,
kindle in us the fire of your Spirit
that with the whole Church on earth and in heaven
we may be made one in him.
Count us worthy
to stand before you as your people
and to offer without ceasing our adoration and service,
through Jesus Christ our Lord.
Through him, with him, and in him,

in the unity of the Holy Spirit,
all honour and glory are yours, Father Almighty,
now and for ever.
All **Amen.**

NOTES

1 This Canon is primarily intended for use on ecumenical occasions, although it may be used at any time.

2 **The Preface.** As far as possible the mighty acts of God are expressed in terms of present activity rather than as past events. At the same time the ideas are borrowed from Scripture, e.g. the reference to creation is borrowed from Acts 17.28.

3 **The Sanctus.** This, with its introduction, has been taken from the Te Deum. Not only is it eminently suitable, but it is supported by the theory expressed by some scholars that this hymn was originally the Preface, Sanctus and Post-sanctus of a Mass for the Easter Vigil (cf. P. Cagin, *Te Deum ou Illatio*, Solesmes 1906; E. Kähler, *Studien zum Te Deum*, Göttingen 1956).

4 **Benedictus.** It is recognized that some people may not wish to use the Benedictus at this point. It may therefore be used at other appropriate points or omitted.

5 **Post-Sanctus.** An unusual feature has been the use of material from the Lord's Prayer at this point: but it is thought to be singularly 'appropriate'.

6 **Institution Narrative.** This is substantially the RSV version of 1 Corinthians 11, and can be regarded as a legitimate scriptural warrant.

7 **The Acclamation.** Doubts have been expressed as to the desirability of placing the Acclamation immediately after the Institution Narrative. Some feel that this puts undue emphasis on the Narrative, implying that this is *the* consecration formula. It seems logical, however, to place the Acclamation at the conclusion of the Anamnesis, providing congregational endorsement of what has just been said.

This particular acclamation is not in common use; and other acclamations may be used in its place.

THE DAILY OFFICE

MORNING OFFICE

The Office begins with *either* a General Sentence *or* a Seasonal Sentence *or* Versicles and Responses.

1 GENERAL SENTENCES

Seek the Lord while he may be found: call upon him while he is near. *Isaiah 55. 6*

God is spirit, and those who worship him must worship in spirit and in truth. *John 4. 24*

In everything make your requests known to God in prayer and petition with thanksgiving. *Philippians 4. 6*

Through Jesus let us continually offer up to God the sacrifice of praise, that is, the tribute of lips which acknowledge his name. *Hebrews 13. 15*

To God, the only God, who saves us through Jesus Christ our Lord, be glory and majesty, dominion and authority, before all time and now and for ever. *Jude 25*

2 SEASONAL SENTENCES

9th before Christmas to the end of 5th before Christmas
Our help is in the name of the Lord, who made heaven and earth. *Psalm 124. 8*

4th before Christmas (Advent 1) to Christmas Eve
The glory of the Lord shall be revealed, and all mankind shall see it. *Isaiah 40. 5*

Christmas Day to the end of Christmas 1
To us a child is born: O come let us adore him. Alleluia! *Isaiah 9. 6*

Christmas 2 to the end of Christmas 6
The grace of God has dawned upon the world with healing for all mankind. *Titus 2. 11*

9th before Easter to the end of 7th before Easter
Jesus said: Come to me, all whose work is hard, whose load is heavy: and I will give you rest. *Matthew 11. 28*

6th before Easter to the end of 3rd before Easter
Jesus said: For their sake I consecrate myself, that they also may be consecrated by the truth. *John 17. 19*

2nd before Easter and Holy Week
Christ the Lord in obedience accepted death—even death on a cross. *Philippians 2. 8*

Easter Week
The Lord is risen indeed. Alleluia! *Luke 24. 34*

Easter 1 to Eve of Ascension
Praise be to the God and Father of our Lord Jesus Christ! In his great mercy he has given us new birth into a living hope by the resurrection of Jesus Christ from the dead. *1 Peter 1. 3*

Ascension to Eve of Pentecost
Since we have a great high priest who has passed into the heavens, Jesus the Son of God, let us with confidence draw near to the throne of grace. *Hebrews 4. 14, 16*

Pentecost to the end of Pentecost 5
Jesus said: You will receive power when the Holy Spirit comes upon you; and then you will be my witnesses. *Acts 1. 8*

Pentecost 6 to the end of Pentecost 10
For anyone who is in Christ, there is a new creation; the old order has gone, and a new order has already begun.
2 Corinthians 5. 17

Pentecost 11 to the end of Pentecost 16
God was in Christ reconciling the world to himself.
2 Corinthians 5. 19

Pentecost 17 to the end of Pentecost season
Jesus said: Know that I am with you always, to the end of time. *Matthew 28. 20*

3 VERSICLES AND RESPONSES

Minister O Lord, open our lips;
People **and our mouth shall proclaim your praise.**
Minister Let us worship the Lord.
People **All praise to his Name.**
All **Glory to the Father, and to the Son,**
and to the Holy Spirit:
as it was in the beginning, is now,
and shall be for ever. Amen.

4 VENITE

O come let us sing out to the Lord:
let us shout in triumph to the rock of our salvation.

Let us come before his face with thanksgiving:
and cry out to him joyfully in psalms.

For the Lord is a great God:
and a great king above all gods.

In his hands are the depths of the earth:
and the peaks of the mountains are his also.

The sea is his and he made it:
his hands moulded dry land.

Come let us worship and bow down:
and kneel before the Lord our maker.

For he himself is our God:
we are the people of his pasture and the sheep of his hand.

If only you would hear his voice today:
for he comes to judge the earth;

He shall judge the world with righteousness:
and the peoples with his truth. (4)

Glory to the Father and to the Son:
and to the Holy Spirit;

as it was in the beginning, is now:
and shall be for ever. Amen.

5 **THE PSALMS**

6 **LESSON** (a) Old Testament
LESSON (b) New Testament

7 **SILENCE**

8 **CANTICLE OR HYMN** (See also Canticles on pp. 70-85)

MONDAY *Te Deum parts 1 and 2*

You are God, we praise you:
you are the Lord and we acclaim you;

you are the eternal Father:
all creation worships you.

To you all angels, all the powers of heaven:
cherubim and seraphim sing in endless praise,

Holy, holy, holy Lord, God of power and might:
heaven and earth are full of your glory.

The glorious company of apostles praise you:
the noble fellowship of prophets praise you,
the white-robed army of martyrs praise you.

Throughout the world the holy Church acclaims you:
Father, of majesty unbounded;

your true and only Son, worthy of all worship:
and the Holy Spirit, advocate and guide.

You, Christ, are the King of glory:
the eternal Son of the Father.

When you became man to set us free:
you did not abhor the Virgin's womb.

You overcame the sting of death:
and opened the kingdom of heaven to all believers.

You are seated at God's right hand in glory:
we believe that you will come, and be our judge.

Come then, Lord, and help your people:
bought with the price of your own blood;

and bring us with your saints:
to glory everlasting. (3)

TUESDAY *A Song of Creation*

Bless the Lord, all created things:
sing his praise and exalt him for ever.

Bless the Lord, you heavens:
sing his praise and exalt him for ever.

Bless the Lord, you angels of the Lord:
bless the Lord, all you his hosts;

bless the Lord, all men on the earth:
sing his praise and exalt him for ever.

O People of God, bless the Lord:
bless the Lord, you priests of the Lord;

bless the Lord, you servants of the Lord:
sing his praise and exalt him for ever.

Bless the Lord, all men of upright spirit:
bless the Lord, you that are holy and humble in heart:

Bless the Father, the Son, and the Holy Spirit:
sing his praise and exalt him for ever.

WEDNESDAY *Benedictus*

Blessed be the Lord, the God of Israel:
for he has come to his people and set them free.

He has raised up for us a mighty saviour:
born of the house of his servant David.

Through his holy prophets he promised of old:
that he would save us from our enemies,
from the hands of all that hate us.

He promised to show mercy to our fathers:
and to remember his holy covenant.

This was the oath he swore to our father Abraham:
to set us free from the hands of our enemies,

free to worship him without fear:
holy and righteous in his sight all the days of our life.

You, my child, shall be called the prophet of the Most High:
for you will go before the Lord to prepare his way,

to give his people knowledge of salvation:
by the forgiveness of all their sins.

In the tender compassion of our God:
the dawn from on high shall break upon us,

to shine upon those who dwell in darkness and the shadow of death:

and to guide our feet into the way of peace. (3)

Glory to the Father and to the Son:
and to the Holy Spirit;

as it was in the beginning, is now:
and shall be for ever. Amen.

THURSDAY *Gloria in excelsis*

Glory to God in the highest,
and peace to his people on earth.

Lord God, heavenly King,
almighty God and Father,
we worship you, we give you thanks,
we praise you for your glory.

Lord Jesus Christ, only Son of the Father,
Lord God, Lamb of God,
you take away the sin of the world:
have mercy on us;
you are seated at the right hand of the Father:
receive our prayer.

For you alone are the Holy One,
you alone are the Lord,
you alone are the Most High,
Jesus Christ, with the Holy Spirit,
in the glory of God the Father. Amen. (3)

FRIDAY *Salvator mundi*

Jesus, Saviour of the world, come to us in your mercy:
we look to you to save and help us.

By your cross and your life laid down you set your people free:
we look to you to save and help us.

When they were ready to perish you saved your disciples:
we look to you to come to our help.

In the greatness of your mercy loose us from our chains:
forgive the sins of all your people.

Make yourself known as our Saviour and mighty Deliverer:
save and help us that we may praise you.

Come now and dwell with us, Lord Christ Jesus:
hear our prayer and be with us always.

And when you come in your glory:
make us to be one with you and to share the life of your kingdom.

SATURDAY *Great and wonderful*

Great and wonderful are your deeds, Lord God the Almighty:
just and true are your ways, O King of the nations.

Who shall not revere and praise your name, O Lord?
for you alone are holy.

All nations shall come and worship in your presence:
for your just dealings have been revealed.

To him who sits on the throne and to the Lamb:
be praise and honour, glory and might, for ever and ever. Amen.

The following is a selection of hymns which may be used in place of the Canticles.

MONDAY	Christ, whose glory fills the skies
TUESDAY	Holy, Holy, Holy, Lord God Almighty
WEDNESDAY	Praise to the Lord, the Almighty, the King of Creation
THURSDAY	Let all the world in every corner sing
FRIDAY	Come let us join our cheerful songs
SATURDAY	Rejoice! the Lord is King

SEASONAL

PRE-CHRISTMAS	The God of Abraham praise
ADVENT	Hark the glad sound! the Saviour comes

CHRISTMAS	O come, all ye faithful
PASSIONTIDE	O sacred head sore wounded
EASTER	Love's redeeming work is done
ASCENSION	Hail the day that sees him rise
PENTECOST	Come down, O Love divine

9 **THE APOSTLES' CREED** (optional)

**I believe in God, the Father almighty,
creator of heaven and earth.**

**I believe in Jesus Christ, his only Son, our Lord.
He was conceived by the power of the Holy Spirit
and born of the Virgin Mary.
He suffered under Pontius Pilate,
was crucified, died, and was buried.
He descended to the dead.
On the third day he rose again.
He ascended into heaven,
and is seated at the right hand of the Father.
He will come again to judge the living and the dead.**

**I believe in the Holy Spirit,
the holy catholic Church,
the communion of saints,
the forgiveness of sins,
the resurrection of the body,
and the life everlasting. Amen.** (3)

10 **THE LORD'S PRAYER**

**Our Father in heaven,
hallowed be your Name,
your kingdom come,
your will be done,
on earth as in heaven.
Give us today our daily bread.
Forgive us our sins
as we forgive those who sin against us.**

Do not bring us to the time of trial
but deliver us from evil.

For the kingdom, the power, and the glory are yours
now and for ever. Amen. (3a)

11 COLLECTS

Of the Day

Morning

Eternal God and Father, you create us by your power and redeem us by your love: guide and strengthen us by your Spirit, that we may give ourselves today in love and service to one another and to you; through Jesus Christ our Lord. **Amen.**

EVENING OFFICE

1 **THE SENTENCES OR VERSICLES AND RESPONSES**

As in the Morning Office.

2 **THE PSALMS**

3 **LESSON** (c) New Testament

4 **SILENCE**

5 **CANTICLE OR HYMN** (See also Canticles on pp. 70-85)

MONDAY *Magnificat*

My soul proclaims the greatness of the Lord:
my spirit rejoices in God my Saviour;

for he has looked in favour on his lowly servant:
from this day all generations will call me blessed.

The Almighty has done great things for me:
and holy is his name.

He has mercy on those who fear him:
in every generation.

He has shown the strength of his arm:
he has scattered the proud in their conceit.

He has cast down the mighty from their thrones:
and has lifted up the lowly.

He has filled the hungry with good things:
and the rich he has sent away empty.

He has come to the help of his servant Israel:
for he has remembered his promise of mercy,

the promise he made to our fathers:
to Abraham and his children for ever. (3)

Glory to the Father and to the Son:
and to the Holy Spirit;

as it was in the beginning, is now:
and shall be for ever. Amen.

TUESDAY *Bless the Lord*

Bless the Lord, the God of our fathers:
bless his holy and glorious name;

bless him in his holy and glorious temple:
sing his praise and exalt him for ever.

Bless him who beholds the depths:
bless him who sits between the cherubim;

bless him on the throne of the kingdom:
sing his praise and exalt him for ever.

Bless him in the heights of heaven:
sing his praise and exalt him for ever.

Bless the Father, the Son, and the Holy Spirit:
sing his praise and exalt him for ever.

WEDNESDAY *Nunc dimittis*

Lord, now you let your servant go in peace:
your word has been fulfilled.

My own eyes have seen the salvation:
which you have prepared in the sight of every people;

a light to reveal you to the nations:
and the glory of your people Israel. (3)

Glory to the Father and to the Son:
and to the Holy Spirit;

as it was in the beginning, is now:
and shall be for ever. Amen.

THURSDAY *Phos hilaron*

O gladsome light, O grace
Of God the Father's face,
The eternal splendour wearing;
Celestial, holy, blest,
Our Saviour Jesus Christ,
Joyful in thine appearing.

Now, ere day fadeth quite,
We see the evening light,
Our wonted hymn outpouring;
Father of might unknown,
Thee, his incarnate Son,
And Holy Spirit adoring.

To thee of right belongs
All praise of holy songs,
O Son of God, lifegiver;
Thee, therefore, O Most High,
The world doth glorify,
And shall exalt for ever. Amen.

FRIDAY *Glory and honour*

Glory and honour and power:
are yours by right, O Lord our God;

for you created all things:
and by your will they have their being.

Glory and honour and power:
are yours by right, O Lamb who was slain;

for by your blood you ransomed men for God:
from every race and language, from every people and nation,

to make them a kingdom of priests:
to stand and serve before our God.

To him who sits on the throne and to the Lamb:
be praise and honour, glory and might, for ever and ever. Amen.

SATURDAY *The Easter Anthems*

Christ our passover has been sacrificed for us:
so let us celebrate the feast,

not with the old leaven of corruption and wickedness:
but with the unleavened bread of sincerity and truth.

Christ once raised from the dead dies no more:
death has no more dominion over him.

In dying he died to sin once for all:
in living he lives to God.

See yourselves therefore as dead to sin:
and alive to God in Jesus Christ our Lord.

Christ has been raised from the dead:
the firstfruits of those who sleep.

For as by man came death:
by man has come also the resurrection of the dead;

for as in Adam all die:
even so in Christ shall all be made alive.

Glory to the Father and to the Son:
and to the Holy Spirit;

as it was in the beginning, is now:
and shall be for ever. Amen.

The following is a selection of hymns which may be used in place of the Canticles.

MONDAY	Now thank we all our God
TUESDAY	O Jesu, King most wonderful (Jesu, the very thought of thee, part 2)
WEDNESDAY	Jesus shall reign where'er the sun
THURSDAY	At the name of Jesus every knee shall bow
FRIDAY	All hail the power of Jesus' name
SATURDAY	Songs of praise the angels sang

SEASONAL

PRE-CHRISTMAS	All creatures of our God and King
ADVENT	O come, O come, Emmanuel
CHRISTMAS	Of the Father's love begotten
PASSIONTIDE	The royal banners forward go
EASTER	Ye choirs of new Jerusalem
ASCENSION	The head that once was crowned with thorns
PENTECOST	Come, Holy Ghost, our souls inspire

6 ACT OF PENITENCE

Let us confess our sins to Almighty God.

**Most merciful God,
we confess that we have sinned against you
in thought, word, and deed.**

**We have not loved you with our whole heart.
We have not loved our neighbours as ourselves.
We pray you of your mercy
to forgive what we have been,
to help us to amend what we are,
and to direct what we shall be;
that we may delight in your will
and walk in your ways;
through Jesus Christ our Lord. Amen.**

Either

Christ Jesus came into the world to save sinners.
Hear then the word of grace and the assurance of pardon:
Your sins are forgiven for his sake.

Or

Almighty God have mercy upon you,
pardon and deliver you from all your sins,
confirm and strengthen you in all goodness,
and keep you in life eternal;
through Jesus Christ our Lord. **Amen.**

7 COLLECT

Lighten our darkness, Lord, we pray; and in your mercy
defend us from all perils and dangers of this night;
for the love of your only Son, our Saviour Jesus Christ. **Amen.**

Here may follow the Thanksgivings or other prayers.

THE SHORT FORM OF THE DAILY OFFICE

If only a single form of the Office is used, it may take the following form:

SENTENCE or VERSICLES AND RESPONSES

PSALM—Morning or Evening

One or two LESSONS

SILENCE

CANTICLE OR HYMN—Morning or Evening

ACT OF PENITENCE

THE LORD'S PRAYER

COLLECT OF THE DAY

The Office may be followed by Intercessions and/or Thanksgivings.

PSALMS FOR THE DAILY OFFICE

9 before Christmas

MONDAY	M	1, 2
	E	3, 4
TUESDAY	M	5, 6
	E	7
WEDNESDAY	M	8, 9
	E	10
THURSDAY	M	11, 12
	E	13, 14
FRIDAY	M	15, 16
	E	17
SATURDAY	M	18. 1-30
	E	18. 31-end

8 before Christmas

MONDAY	M	19
	E	20, 21
TUESDAY	M	22
	E	23, 24
WEDNESDAY	M	25
	E	26, 27
THURSDAY	M	28, 29
	E	30
FRIDAY	M	31
	E	32
SATURDAY	M	33
	E	34

7 before Christmas

MONDAY	M	35
	E	36
TUESDAY	M	37. 1-22
	E	37. 23-end
WEDNESDAY	M	38
	E	39
THURSDAY	M	40
	E	41
FRIDAY	M	42, 43
	E	44
SATURDAY	M	45, 46
	E	47, 48

6 before Christmas

MONDAY	M	49
	E	50
TUESDAY	M	51
	E	52, 53
WEDNESDAY	M	54, 55
	E	56, 57
THURSDAY	M	(58), 59
	E	60, 61
FRIDAY	M	62, 63
	E	64, 65
SATURDAY	M	66, 67
	E	68

5 before Christmas

MONDAY	M	69
	E	70, 71
TUESDAY	M	72
	E	73
WEDNESDAY	M	74
	E	75, 76
THURSDAY	M	77
	E	78. 1-40
FRIDAY	M	78. 41-end
	E	79
SATURDAY	M	80
	E	81

4 before Christmas (Advent 1)

MONDAY	M	82, 83
	E	84, 85
TUESDAY	M	86
	E	87, 88
WEDNESDAY	M	89. 1-36
	E	89. 37-end
THURSDAY	M	90
	E	91
FRIDAY	M	92, 93
	E	94
SATURDAY	M	95 (*or* 100), 96
	E	97, 98

3 before Christmas (Advent 2)

MONDAY	M	99, 100 (*or* 95), 101
	E	102
TUESDAY	M	103
	E	104
WEDNESDAY	M	105. 1-22
	E	105. 23-end
THURSDAY	M	106. 1-23
	E	106. 24-end
FRIDAY	M	107. 1-22
	E	107. 23-end
SATURDAY	M	108, (109), 110
	E	111, 112, 113

2 before Christmas (Advent 3)

MONDAY	M	114, 115
	E	116, 117
TUESDAY	M	118
	E	119. 1-24
WEDNESDAY	M	119. 25-40
	E	119. 41-56
THURSDAY	M	119. 57-72
	E	119. 73-88
FRIDAY	M	119. 89-104
	E	119. 105-128
SATURDAY	M	119. 129-152
	E	119. 153-end

1 before Christmas (Advent 4)

MONDAY	M	120, 121
	E	122, 123
TUESDAY	M	124, 125
	E	126, 127
WEDNESDAY	M	128, 129
	E	130, 131
THURSDAY	M	132
	E	133, 134
FRIDAY	M	135
	E	136
SATURDAY	M	137, 138
	E	139

Christmas Day

M 19
E 8, 110

December 26

M 13, 46
E 57, 86

December 27

M 97
E 21

December 28

M 36
E 124, 128

December 29

M 140
E 141

December 30

M 142
E 143

December 31

M 144
E 145

January 1

M 115
E 148

January 2

M 146
E 147

Christmas 1

MONDAY	M	26, (27)
	E	28, 29
TUESDAY	M	30
	E	31
WEDNESDAY	M	32
	E	33
THURSDAY	M	34
	E	35
FRIDAY	M	36
	E	37. 1-22
SATURDAY	M	37. 23-end
	E	38

Christmas 2

MONDAY	M	39
	E	40
TUESDAY	M	41
	E	42, 43
WEDNESDAY	M	44
	E	45, 46
THURSDAY	M	47, 48
	E	49
FRIDAY	M	50
	E	51
SATURDAY	M	52, 53
	E	54, 55

Christmas 3

MONDAY	M	56, 57
	E	(58), 59
TUESDAY	M	60, 61
	E	62, 63
WEDNESDAY	M	64, 65
	E	66, 67
THURSDAY	M	68
	E	69
FRIDAY	M	70, 71
	E	72
SATURDAY	M	73
	E	74

Christmas 4

MONDAY	M	75, 76
	E	77
TUESDAY	M	78. 1-40
	E	78. 41-end
WEDNESDAY	M	79
	E	80
THURSDAY	M	81
	E	82, 83
FRIDAY	M	84, 85
	E	86
SATURDAY	M	87, 88
	E	89. 1-36

Christmas 5

MONDAY	M	89. 37-end
	E	90
TUESDAY	M	91
	E	92, 93
WEDNESDAY	M	94
	E	95 (*or* 100), 96
THURSDAY	M	97, 98
	E	99, 100 (*or* 95), 101
FRIDAY	M	102
	E	103
SATURDAY	M	104
	E	105. 1-22

Christmas 6

MONDAY	M	105. 23-end
	E	106. 1-23
TUESDAY	M	106. 24-end
	E	107. 1-22
WEDNESDAY	M	107. 23-end
	E	108, (109)
THURSDAY	M	110, 111
	E	112, 113
FRIDAY	M	114
	E	115
SATURDAY	M	116, 117
	E	118

If further weeks after Christmas are required, the psalms for the weeks of Pentecost 3 and 4 may be used.

9 before Easter

MONDAY	M	1, 2, 3
	E	4, 5, 6
TUESDAY	M	7
	E	8, 9
WEDNESDAY	M	10
	E	11, 12
THURSDAY	M	13, 14
	E	15, 16
FRIDAY	M	17
	E	18. 1-30
SATURDAY	M	18. 31-end
	E	19

8 before Easter

MONDAY	M	20, 21
	E	22
TUESDAY	M	23, 24
	E	25
WEDNESDAY	M	26, 27
	E	28, 29
THURSDAY	M	30
	E	31
FRIDAY	M	32
	E	33
SATURDAY	M	34
	E	35

7 before Easter

MONDAY	M	36
	E	37. 1-22
TUESDAY	M	37. 23-end
	E	39
Ash Wednesday	M	102
	E	38
THURSDAY	M	40
	E	41
FRIDAY	M	42, 43
	E	44
SATURDAY	M	45, 46
	E	47, 48

6 before Easter (Lent 1)

MONDAY	M	49
	E	50
TUESDAY	M	51
	E	52, 53
WEDNESDAY	M	54, 55
	E	56, 57
THURSDAY	M	(58), 59
	E	60, 61
FRIDAY	M	62, 63
	E	64, 65
SATURDAY	M	66, 67
	E	68

5 before Easter (Lent 2)

MONDAY	M	69
	E	70, 71
TUESDAY	M	72
	E	73
WEDNESDAY	M	74
	E	75, 76
THURSDAY	M	77
	E	78. 1-40
FRIDAY	M	78. 41-end
	E	79
SATURDAY	M	80
	E	81

4 before Easter (Lent 3)

MONDAY	M	82, 83
	E	84, 85
TUESDAY	M	86
	E	87, 88
WEDNESDAY	M	89. 1-36
	E	89. 37-end
THURSDAY	M	90
	E	91
FRIDAY	M	92, 93
	E	94
SATURDAY	M	95 (*or* 100), 96
	E	97, 98

3 before Easter (Lent 4)

MONDAY	M	99, 100 (*or* 95), 101
	E	102
TUESDAY	M	103
	E	104
WEDNESDAY	M	105. 1-22
	E	105. 23-end
THURSDAY	M	106. 1-23
	E	106. 24-end
FRIDAY	M	107. 1-22
	E	107. 23-end
SATURDAY	M	108, (109)
	E	111, 112, 113

2 before Easter (Passion Sunday)

MONDAY	M	114, 115
	E	116, 117
TUESDAY	M	118
	E	119. 1-24
WEDNESDAY	M	119. 25-40
	E	119. 41-56
THURSDAY	M	119. 57-72
	E	119. 73-88
FRIDAY	M	119. 89-104
	E	119. 105-128
SATURDAY	M	119. 129-152
	E	119. 153-end

1 before Easter (Palm Sunday)

	M	61, 62
	E	22. 1-21

Holy Week
(Psalms in brackets may be omitted)

MONDAY	M	13, (26)
	E	27, (28)
TUESDAY	M	64 *or* 88
	E	31
WEDNESDAY	M	41, 42, (43)
	E	55
THURSDAY	M	54, (64)
	E	69. 1-21, 29-36
Good Friday	M	22
	E	40
SATURDAY	M	23, (30)
	E	(116), 142

Easter

MONDAY	M	120, 121
	E	122, 123
TUESDAY	M	124, 125
	E	126, 127
WEDNESDAY	M	128, 129
	E	130, 131
THURSDAY	M	132
	E	133, 134
FRIDAY	M	135
	E	136
SATURDAY	M	137, 138
	E	139

Easter 1

Monday	M	140
	E	141
Tuesday	M	142, 143
	E	144
Wednesday	M	145
	E	146, 147
Thursday	M	148
	E	149, 150
Friday	M	1, 2
	E	3, 4
Saturday	M	5, 6
	E	7

Easter 2

Monday	M	8, 9
	E	10
Tuesday	M	11, 12
	E	13, 14
Wednesday	M	15, 16
	E	17
Thursday	M	18. 1-30
	E	18. 31-end
Friday	M	19
	E	20, 21
Saturday	M	22
	E	23, 24

Easter 3

Monday	M	25
	E	26, 27
Tuesday	M	28, 29
	E	30
Wednesday	M	31
	E	32
Thursday	M	33
	E	34
Friday	H	35
	E	36
Saturday	M	37. 1-22
	E	37. 23-end

Easter 4

Monday	M	38
	E	39
Tuesday	M	40
	E	41
Wednesday	M	42, 43
	E	44
Thursday	M	45, 46
	E	47, 48
Friday	M	49
	E	50
Saturday	M	51
	E	52, 53

Easter 5

Monday	M	54, 55
	E	56, 57
Tuesday	M	(58), 59
	E	60, 61
Wednesday	M	62, 63
	E	64, 65
Ascension	M	96, 97
Day	E	15, 24
Friday	M	66, 67
	E	68
Saturday	M	69
	E	70, 71

Easter 6

Monday	M	72
	E	73
Tuesday	M	74
	E	75, 76
Wednesday	M	77
	E	78. 1-40
Thursday	M	78. 41-end
	E	79
Friday	M	80
	E	81
Saturday	M	82, 83
	E	84, 85

Pentecost

MONDAY	M	86
	E	87, 88
TUESDAY	M	89. 1-36
	E	89. 37-end
WEDNESDAY	M	90
	E	91
THURSDAY	M	92, 93
	E	94
FRIDAY	M	95 (*or* 100), 96
	E	97, 98
SATURDAY	M	99, 100 (*or* 95), 101
	E	102

Pentecost 1

MONDAY	M	103
	E	104
TUESDAY	M	105. 1-22
	E	105. 23-end
WEDNESDAY	M	106. 1-23
	E	106. 24-end
THURSDAY	M	107. 1-22
	E	107. 23-end
FRIDAY	M	108, (109)
	E	110, 111
SATURDAY	M	112, 113
	E	114

Pentecost 2

MONDAY	M	115
	E	116, 117
TUESDAY	M	118
	E	119. 1-24
WEDNESDAY	M	119. 25-40
	E	119. 41-56
THURSDAY	M	119. 57-72
	E	119. 73-88
FRIDAY	M	119. 89-104
	E	119. 105-128
SATURDAY	M	119. 129-152
	E	119. 153-end

Pentecost 3

MONDAY	M	120, 121
	E	122, 123
TUESDAY	M	124, 125
	E	126, 127
WEDNESDAY	M	128, 129
	E	130, 131
THURSDAY	M	132
	E	133, 134
FRIDAY	M	135
	E	136
SATURDAY	M	137, 138
	E	139

Pentecost 4

MONDAY	M	140
	E	141
TUESDAY	M	142
	E	143
WEDNESDAY	M	144
	E	145
THURSDAY	M	146, 147
	E	148
FRIDAY	M	149, 150
	E	1, 2
SATURDAY	M	3, 4
	E	5, 6

Pentecost 5

MONDAY	M	7
	E	8, 9
TUESDAY	M	10
	E	11, 12
WEDNESDAY	M	13, 14
	E	15, 16
THURSDAY	M	17
	E	18. 1-30
FRIDAY	M	18. 31-end
	E	19
SATURDAY	M	20, 21
	E	22

Pentecost 6

MONDAY	M	23, 24
	E	25
TUESDAY	M	26, 27
	E	28, 29
WEDNESDAY	M	30
	E	31
THURSDAY	M	32
	E	33
FRIDAY	M	34
	E	35
SATURDAY	M	36
	E	37. 1-22

Pentecost 7

MONDAY	M	37. 23-end
	E	38
TUESDAY	M	39
	E	40
WEDNESDAY	M	41
	E	42, 43
THURSDAY	M	44
	E	45, 46
FRIDAY	M	47, 48
	E	49
SATURDAY	M	50
	E	51

Pentecost 8

MONDAY	M	52, 53
	E	54, 55
TUESDAY	M	56, 57
	E	(58), 59
WEDNESDAY	M	60, 61
	E	62, 63
THURSDAY	M	64, 65
	E	66, 67
FRIDAY	M	68
	E	69
SATURDAY	M	70, 71
	E	72

Pentecost 9

MONDAY	M	73
	E	74
TUESDAY	M	75, 76
	E	77
WEDNESDAY	M	78. 1-40
	E	78. 41-end
THURSDAY	M	79
	E	80
FRIDAY	M	81
	E	82, 83
SATURDAY	M	84, 85
	E	86

Pentecost 10

MONDAY	M	87, 88
	E	89. 1-36
TUESDAY	M	89. 37-end
	E	90
WEDNESDAY	M	91
	E	92, 93
THURSDAY	M	94
	E	95 (*or* 100), 96
FRIDAY	M	97, 98
	E	99, 100 (*or* 95), 101
SATURDAY	M	102
	E	103

Pentecost 11

MONDAY	M	104
	E	105. 1-22
TUESDAY	M	105. 23-end
	E	106. 1-23
WEDNESDAY	M	106. 24-end
	E	107. 1-22
THURSDAY	M	107. 23-end
	E	108, (109)
FRIDAY	M	110, 111
	E	112, 113
SATURDAY	M	114
	E	115

Pentecost 12

MONDAY	M	116, 117
	E	118
TUESDAY	M	119. 1-24
	E	119. 25-40
WEDNESDAY	M	119. 41-56
	E	119. 57-72
THURSDAY	M	119. 73-88
	E	119. 89-104
FRIDAY	M	119. 105-128
	E	119. 129-152
SATURDAY	M	119. 153-end
	E	120, 121

Pentecost 13

MONDAY	M	122, 123
	E	124, 125
TUESDAY	M	126, 127
	E	128, 129
WEDNESDAY	M	130, 131
	E	132
THURSDAY	M	133, 134
	E	135
FRIDAY	M	136
	E	137, 138
SATURDAY	M	139
	E	140, 141

Pentecost 14

MONDAY	M	142, 143
	E	144
TUESDAY	M	145
	E	146, 147
WEDNESDAY	M	148
	E	149, 150
THURSDAY	M	1, 2, 3
	E	4, 5, 6
FRIDAY	M	7
	E	8, 9
SATURDAY	M	10
	E	11, 12

Pentecost 15

MONDAY	M	13, 14
	E	15, 16
TUESDAY	M	17
	E	18. 1-30
WEDNESDAY	M	18. 31-end
	E	19
THURSDAY	M	20, 21
	E	22
FRIDAY	M	23, 24
	E	25
SATURDAY	M	26, 27
	E	28, 29

Pentecost 16

MONDAY	M	30
	E	31
TUESDAY	M	32
	E	33
WEDNESDAY	M	34
	E	35
THURSDAY	M	36
	E	37. 1-22
FRIDAY	M	37. 23-end
	E	38
SATURDAY	M	39
	E	40

Pentecost 17

MONDAY	M	41
	E	42, 43
TUESDAY	M	44
	E	45, 46
WEDNESDAY	M	47, 48
	E	49
THURSDAY	M	50
	E	51
FRIDAY	M	52, 53
	E	54, 55
SATURDAY	M	56, 57
	E	(58), 59

Pentecost 18

MONDAY	M	60, 61
	E	62, 63
TUESDAY	M	64, 65
	E	66, 67
WEDNESDAY	M	68
	E	69
THURSDAY	M	70, 71
	E	72
FRIDAY	M	73
	E	74
SATURDAY	M	75, 76
	E	77

Pentecost 19

MONDAY	M	78. 1-40
	E	78. 41-end
TUESDAY	M	79
	E	80
WEDNESDAY	M	81
	E	82, 83
THURSDAY	M	84, 85
	E	86
FRIDAY	M	87, 88
	E	89. 1-36
SATURDAY	M	89. 37-end
	E	90

Pentecost 20

MONDAY	M	91
	E	92, 93
TUESDAY	M	94
	E	95 (*or* 100), 96
WEDNESDAY	M	97
	E	98
THURSDAY	M	99, 100 (*or* 95), 101
	E	102
FRIDAY	M	103
	E	104
SATURDAY	M	105. 1-22
	E	105. 23-end

Pentecost 21

MONDAY	M	106. 1-23
	E	106. 24-end
TUESDAY	M	107. 1-22
	E	107. 23-end
WEDNESDAY	M	108, (109)
	E	110, 111
THURSDAY	M	112, 113
	E	114
FRIDAY	M	115
	E	116, 117
SATURDAY	M	118
	E	119. 1-24

If further weeks after Pentecost 21 are required, the psalms for the weeks of Pentecost 3 and 4 may be used.

LECTIONARY FOR THE DAILY OFFICE

FIRST YEAR

	Lesson (a)		Lesson (b)		Lesson (c)	
9 before Christmas						
M	Gen.	1. 1-19	John	1. 1-18	Rev.	1. 1-8
Tu		1. 20 – 2. 3		1. 19-34		1. 9-20
W		2. 4-25		1. 35-51		2. 1-11
T		3. 1-15		2. 1-12		2. 12-17
F		3. 16-24		2. 13-25		2. 18-29
Sa		4. 1-16		3. 1-21		3. 1-6
8 before Christmas						
M	Gen.	6. 9-22	John	3. 22-36	Rev.	3. 7-13
Tu		7. 6-24		4. 1-26		3. 14-22
W		8. 1-12		4. 27-42		4
T		8. 13-22		4. 43-54		5
F		9. 1-17		5. 1-18		6. 1-8
Sa		11. 1-9		5. 19-47		6. 9-17
7 before Christmas						
M	Gen.	12. 1 – 13. 1	John	6. 1-15	Rev.	7. 1-8
Tu		13. 2-18		6. 16-29		7. 9-17
W		15. 1-6		6. 30-40		8. 1-13
T		17. 1-14		6. 41-58		9. 1-12
F		18. 1-15		6. 59-71		9. 13-21
Sa		18. 16-33		7. 1-13		10. 1-11
6 before Christmas						
M	Gen.	21. 1-21	John	7. 14-24	Rev.	11. 1-13
Tu		22. 1-19		7. 25-36		11. 14-19
W		24. 1-27		7. 37-52		12. 1-6
T		24. 28-51		8. 1-11		12. 7-12
F		24. 52-67		8. 12-30		12. 13-17
Sa		25. 19-34		8. 31-47		13. 1-10

	Lesson (a)	Lesson (b)	Lesson (c)
5 before Christmas			
M	Gen. 27. 1-29	John 8. 48-59	Rev. 13.11-18
Tu	27. 30-45	9. 1-12	14. 1-13
W	28. 10-22	9. 13-29	14. 14-20
T	29. 1-30	9. 30-41	15
F	32. 1-23	10. 1-21	16. 1-11
Sa	32. 24 – 33. 11	10. 22-42	16. 12-21
4 before Christmas (Advent 1)			
M	Isa. 1. 1-9	Rev. 17. 1-6	Matt. 23. 1-12
Tu	1. 10-20	17. 7-18	23. 13-22
W	1. 21-31	19. 1-10	23. 23-28
T	2. 1-11	19. 11-16 (or – 21)	23. 29-39
F	2. 12-22	20. 1-10	24. 1-14
Sa	3. 1-8	20. 11-15	24. 15-28
3 before Christmas (Advent 2)			
M	Isa. 3. 13 – 4. 1	Rev. 21. 1-8	Matt. 24. 29-34
Tu	4. 2-6	21. 9-14	24. 35-42
W	5. 1-7	21. 15-21	24. 43-51
T	5. 8-23	21. 22 – 22. 5	25. 1-13
F	5. 24-30	22. 6-13	25. 14-30
Sa	6. 1-12	22. 14-21	25. 31-46
2 before Christmas (Advent 3)			
M	1 Kgs. 17. 1-16	Col. 1. 1-14	Luke 1. 5-25
Tu	18. 1-16	1. 15-29	3. 1-14
W	18. 17-29	2. 1-15	3.15-22
T	18. 30-46	2. 16 – 3. 11	Matt. 11. 2-6
F	19. 1-8	3. 12-25	11. 7-19
Sa	19. 9-21	4	John 5. 30-36

These are John Baptist passages.
Readings for 18-31 Dec. will take priority.

	Lesson (a)	Lesson (b)	Lesson (c)
Weekdays 18-31 December			
18	Isa. 7. 10-17	Luke 1. 26-38	Philemon
19	28. 14-22	1. 39-45	2 John
20	29. 13-24	1. 46-56*	3 John
21	30. 15-21	1. 57-66	Phil. 1. 1-8
22	32. 1-8	1. 67-80	1. 9-18
23	35	Matt. 3. 1-10*	1. 19-26
24	52. 1-10	1. 18-25	1. 27 – 2. 4
Christmas Day	65. 17-25	Luke 2. 15-20	Phil. 2. 5-11
26	40. 1-11	2. 21-25	2. 12-18
27	40. 12-24	2. 25-35	2. 19-30
28	40. 25-31	2. 36-40	3. 1-11
29	41. 1-13	Matt. 2. 1-12	3. 12 – 4. 1
30	41. 14-20	2. 13-23	4. 2-9
31	Deut. 11. 11-21	Luke 2. 41-52	4. 10-20

*Either of these lessons may be omitted instead of that provided for the date of the Sunday (1st before Christmas), and the remaining lessons read in sequence on weekdays.

	Lesson (a)	Lesson (b)	Lesson (c)
Christmas 1			
M	Isa. 42. 1-9	Eph. 1. 1-14	Matt. 3
Tu	42. 10-25	1. 15-23	4. 1-11
W	43. 1-7	2. 1-10	4. 12-25
T	43. 8-21	2. 11-22	5. 1-12
F	43. 22-28	3. 1-13	5. 13-20
Sa	44. 1-5	3. 14-21	5. 21-26

Readings for 18-31 December will take priority.

		Lesson (a)		Lesson (b)		Lesson (c)
Christmas 2						
M	Isa.	44. 6-22	Eph.	4. 1-16	Matt.	5. 27-37
Tu		44. 23-28		4. 17-32		5. 38-48
W		45. 1-8		5. 1-14		6. 1-15
T		45. 9-13		5. 15-33		6. 16-34
F		45. 14-17		6. 1-9		7. 1-12
Sa		45. 18-25		6. 10-24		7. 13-29
Christmas 3						
M	Isa.	46	1 Tim.	1. 1-17	Matt.	8. 1-13
Tu		47. 1-9		1. 18 – 2. 5		8. 14-22
W		47. 10-15		3		8. 23-34
T		48. 1-11		4		9. 1-8
F		48. 12-22		5. 1-16		9. 9-17
Sa		49. 1-6		5. 17-25		9. 18-26
Christmas 4						
M	Isa.	49. 7-13	1 Tim.	6. 1-10	Matt.	9. 27-38
Tu		49. 14-21		6. 11-21		10. 1-8
W		49. 22-26	2 Tim.	1. 1-14		10. 9-15
T		50		1. 15 – 2. 13		10. 16-23
F		51. 1-11		2. 14-26		10. 24-33
Sa		51. 12-23		3		10. 34 – 11. 1
Christmas 5						
M	Isa.	52. 13 – 53. 6	2 Tim.	4. 1-18	Matt.	11. 2-6
Tu		53. 7-12	Tit.	1		11. 7-19
W		54. 1-10		2		11. 20-30
T		54. 11-17		3		12. 1-8
F		56. 1-8	1 John	1. 1 – 2. 6		12. 9-21
Sa		57. 15-19		2. 7-17		12. 22-37

	Lesson (a)		Lesson (b)		Lesson (c)	
Christmas 6						
M	Isa.	58. 1-5	1 John.	2. 18-29	Matt.	12. 38-50
Tu		58. 6-12		3. 1-10		13. 1-9
W		58. 13-14		3. 11-24		13. 10-23
T		59. 1-8		4		13. 24-33
F		59. 9-15a		5. 1-12		13. 34-43
Sa		59. 15b-21		5. 13-21		13. 44-58
9 before Easter						
M	Jer.	1. 1-10	Matt.	14. 1-12	Gal.	1. 1-10
Tu		1. 11-19		14. 13-21		1. 11-24
W		2. 4-13		14. 22-36		2. 1-10
T		3. 6-18		15. 1-20		2. 11-21
F		4. 5-14		15. 21-28		3. 1-14
Sa		4. 19-31		15. 29-39		3. 15-22
8 before Easter						
M	Jer.	5. 1-9	Matt.	16. 1-12	Gal.	3. 23-29
Tu		5. 20-31		16. 13-20		4. 1-11
W		6. 9-15		16. 21-28		4. 12-20
T		6. 22-30		17. 1-13		4. 21 – 5. 1
F		7. 1-15		17. 14-27		5. 2-12
Sa		7. 21-28		18. 1-20		5. 13-25
7 before Easter						
M	Jer.	8. 18 – 9. 3	Matt.	18. 21-35	Gal.	6. 1-10
Tu		9. 17-24		19. 1-15		6. 11-18
Ash Wed		14. 7-9	Mark	2. 13-22	2 Cor.	7. 2-10
T		10. 1-10	Matt.	19. 16-30	Jas.	1. 1-11
F		10. 11-16		20. 1-16		1. 12-27
Sa		10. 17-24		20. 17-28		2. 1-13

		Lesson (a)		Lesson (b)		Lesson (c)

6 before Easter (Lent 1)

M	Jer.	12. 1-6	Matt.	20. 29-34	Jas.	2. 14-26
Tu		13. 20-27		21. 1-11		3. 1-12
W		15. 10-21		21. 12-17		3. 13-18
T		17. 9-18		21. 18-32		4. 1-12
F		18. 1-12		21. 33-46		4. 13 – 5. 6
Sa		18. 13-23		22. 1-14		5. 7-20

5 before Easter (Lent 2)

M	Jer.	19. 1-13	Heb.	1	Matt.	22. 15-22
Tu		19. 14 – 20. 6		2. 1-9		22. 23-33
W		20. 7-18		2. 10-18		22. 34-46
T		21. 1-10		3. 1-6		23. 1-12
F		22. 13-19		3. 7-19		23. 13-24
Sa		22. 20-30		4. 1-10		23. 25-39

4 before Easter (Lent 3)

M	Jer.	23. 1-8	Heb.	4. 11-16	Matt.	24. 1-14
Tu		23. 16-29		5. 1-10		24. 15-28
W		24		5. 11 – 6. 8		24. 29-34
T		25. 1-14		6. 9-20		24. 35-51
F		26. 1-9		7. 1-10		25. 1-13
Sa		26. 10-24		7. 11-28		25. 14-30

3 before Easter (Lent 4)

M	Jer.	29. 1, 4-14	Heb.	8	Matt.	25. 31-46
Tu		30. 10-22		9. 1-14		26. 1-13
W		31. 1-14		9. 15-28		26. 14-29
T		31. 15-22		10. 1-18		26. 30-35
F		31. 23-34		10. 19-39		26. 36-46
Sa		31. 35-40		11. 1-12		26. 47-56

		Lesson (a)		Lesson (b)		Lesson (c)
2 before Easter (Passion Sunday)						
M	Jer.	32. 1-15	Heb.	11. 13-22	Matt.	26. 57-68
Tu		36. 1-8, 27-32		11. 23-31		26. 69-75
W		37. 11-21		11. 32-40		27. 1-10
T		38. 1-13		12. 1-11		27. 11-26
F		39		12. 12-29		27. 27-44
Sa		42. 1-12		13. 1-21		27. 45-66
1 before Easter (Palm Sunday)						
Holy Week						
M	Lam.	1. 1-11	Gal.	6. 11-18	John	14. 1-11
Tu		2. 11-17	Rom.	5. 6-11		14. 12-31
W		3. 40-51		5. 12-19		15. 1-17
T	Exod.	24. 1-11	Eph.	2. 11-18		15. 18-27
Good Fri	Lam.	5. 15-22	Col.	1. 18-23	Mark	15. 21-41
Sa	Gen.	7. 11-18	1 John	5. 4-10		15. 42-47
Easter Week						
M	Isa.	26. 1-9	Mark	16. 9-18	1 Pet.	1. 1-12
Tu		26. 13-19	Luke	24. 1-12		1. 13-25
W	2 Kgs.	4. 18-37		24. 13-35		2. 1-10
T	Ezek.	37. 1-14		24. 36-49		2. 11-25
F	Zech.	8. 1-8	Matt.	28. 1-10		3. 1-12
Sa	Zeph.	3. 14-20		28. 11-20		3. 13-22
Easter 1						
M	Exod.	1	Mark	1. 1-13	1 Pet.	4. 1-11
Tu		2		1. 14-20		4. 12-19
W		3. 1-12		1. 21-28		5
T		3. 13-22		1. 29-39	2 Pet.	1. 1-11
F		4. 1-17		1. 40-45		1. 12-21
Sa		4. 18-31		2. 1-12		3. 8-13

		Lesson (a)		Lesson (b)		Lesson (c)
Easter 2						
M	Exod.	5. 1-14	Mark	2. 13-17	1 Thess.	1
Tu		5. 15-23		2. 18-22		2. 1-12
W		6. 1-13		2. 23-28		2. 13-20
T		6. 28 – 7. 13		3. 1-6		3
F		7. 14-24		3. 7-19a		4. 1-12
Sa		7. 25 – 8. 15		3. 19b-30		4. 13-18
Easter 3						
M	Exod.	8. 16-32	Mark	3. 31-35		5. 1-11
Tu		9. 1-12		4. 1-20		5. 12-28
W		9. 13-35		4. 21-34	2 Thess.	1
T		10. 1-11		4. 35-41		2. 1-12
F		10. 12-29		5. 1-20		2. 13-17
Sa		11		5. 21-34		3
Easter 4						
M	Exod.	12. 1-13	Mark	5. 35-43	Rom.	1. 1-17
Tu		12. 14-27		6. 1-6		1. 18-32
W		12. 28-36		6. 7-13		2. 1-16
T		12. 37-51		6. 14-29		2. 17-29
F		13. 1-16		6. 30-44		3. 1-20
Sa		13. 17 – 14. 4		6. 45-56		3. 21-31
Easter 5						
M	Exod.	14. 5-20	Mark	7. 1-13	Rom.	4. 1-12
Tu		14. 21-31		7. 14-23		4. 13-25
W		15. 22-27		7. 24-30		5. 1-11
Ascension Day	2 Kgs.	2. 1-15		16. 14-20	Heb.	9. 11-15
F	Exod.	16. 1-21		7. 31-37	Rom.	5. 12-21
Sa		16. 22-35		8. 1-10		6. 1-14

		Lesson (a)		Lesson (b)		Lesson (c)
Easter 6						
M	Exod.	17	Mark	8. 11-21	Rom.	6. 15-23
Tu		18. 1-12		8. 22-26		7. 1-12
W		18. 13-27		8. 27-33		7. 13-25
T		19. 1-14		8. 34 – 9. 1		8. 1-17
F		19. 16-25		9. 2-13		8. 18-30
Sa		20. 1-17		9. 14-29		8. 31-39
Pentecost						
M	Num.	11. 16-30	Rom.	9. 1-13	John	14. 1-11
Tu	1 Sam.	10. 1-10		9. 14-29		14. 12-31
W	Ezek.	11. 14-20		9. 30 – 10. 10		15. 1-17
T	Mic.	3. 1-8		10. 11-21		15. 18-27
F	Isa.	61. 1-7		11. 1-24		16. 1-15
Sa	Jer.	31. 31-34		11. 25-36		16. 16-33
Pentecost 1						
M	Exod.	20. 18-26	Rom.	12. 1-8	Mark	9. 30-37
Tu		24. 1-8		12. 9-21		9. 38-50
W		24. 9-18		13. 1-14		10. 1-12
T		32. 1-14		14. 1-12		10. 13-22
F		32. 15-29		14. 13-23		10. 23-31
Sa		34. 1-10		15. 1-13		10. 32-45
Pentecost 2						
M	Num.	9. 15-23	Rom.	15. 14-21	Mark	10. 46-52
Tu		12		15. 22-33		11. 1-11
W		13. 17-33	Acts	1. 1-14		11. 12-19
T		14. 1-10a		1. 15-26		11. 20-26
F		14. 10b-25		2. 1-13		11. 27-33
Sa		20. 1-13		2. 14-36		12. 1-12

		Lesson (a)		Lesson (b)		Lesson (c)
Pentecost 3						
M	Num.	21. 4-9	Acts	2. 37-47	Mark	12. 13-17
Tu		22. 2-15, 21-35		3. 1-10		12. 18-27
W		22. 36 – 23. 12		3. 11 – 4. 4		12. 28-34
T		23. 13-30		4. 5-22		12. 35-44
F		24. 1-9		4. 23-31		13. 1-13
Sa		24. 10-25		4. 32 – 5. 11		13. 14-27
Pentecost 4						
M	Deut.	1. 1-8	Acts	5. 12-26	Mark	13. 28-37
Tu		4. 1-13		5. 27-42		14. 1-9
W		4. 14-24		6		14. 10-25
T		4. 25-35		7. 1-16		14. 26-42
F		5. 1-21		7. 17-36		14. 43-52
Sa		5. 22-33		7. 37-53		14. 53-65
Pentecost 5						
M	Deut.	6. 1-12	Acts	7. 54 – 8. 3	Mark	14. 66-72
Tu		6. 13-25		8. 4-25		15. 1-15
W		7. 6-11		8. 26-40		15. 16-32
T		8. 1-10		9. 1-19a		15. 33-47
F		8. 11-20		9. 19b-31		16. 1-8
Sa		9. 1-5		9. 32-43		16. 9-20
Pentecost 6						
M	Deut.	10. 11-22	Luke	1. 1-25	Acts	10. 1-16
Tu		11. 1-12		1. 26-38		10. 17-33
W		12. 1-11		1. 39-56		10. 34-48
T		13. 1-5		1. 57-66		11. 1-18
F		15. 1-11		1. 67-80		11. 19-30
Sa		18. 15-22		2. 1-7		12. 1-11

		Lesson (a)		Lesson (b)		Lesson (c)
Pentecost 7						
M	Deut.	26. 1-11	Luke	2. 8-20	Acts	12. 12-25
Tu		28. 1-14		2. 21-32		13. 1-12
W		30. 1-10		2. 33-40		13. 13-41
T		30. 11-20		2. 41-52		13. 42 – 14. 7
F		32. 1-12		3. 1-14		14. 8-28
Sa		34		3. 15-22		15. 1-21
Pentecost 8						
M	Josh.	1. 1-11	Luke	4. 1-13	Acts	15. 22-35
Tu		2		4. 14-30		15. 36 – 16. 5
W		3. 7-17		4. 31-44		16. 6-24
T		4. 1-11		5. 1-11		16. 25-40
F		5. 13 – 6. 11		5. 12-26		17. 1-15
Sa		6. 12-23		5. 27-39		17. 16-34
Pentecost 9						
M	Josh.	7. 1-15	Luke	6. 1-11	Acts	18. 1-21
Tu		7. 16-26		6. 12-26		18. 22 – 19. 7
W		8. 10-23		6. 27-38		19. 8-20
T		9. 3-21		6. 39-49		19. 21-41
F		24. 1-13		7. 1-10		20. 1-16
Sa		24. 14-25		7. 11-23		20. 17-38
Pentecost 10						
M	Judg.	2. 11-23	Luke	7. 24-35	Acts	21. 1-16
Tu		4. 1-21		7. 36-50		21. 17-26
W		5. 1-18		8. 1-15		21. 27-39
T		5. 19-31		8. 16-25		21. 40 – 22. 21
F		6. 1, 11-32		8. 26-39		22. 22 – 23. 11
Sa		7. 1-23		8. 40-56		23. 12-35

		Lesson (a)		Lesson (b)		Lesson (c)
Pentecost 11						
M	Judg.	9. 1-21	Luke	9. 1-9	Acts	24. 1-23
Tu		9. 44-57		9. 10-17		24. 24 – 25. 12
W		11. 1-6, 29-40		9. 18-27		25. 13-27
T		13		9. 28-36		26. 1-23
F		14. 1-14		9. 37-43a		26. 24-32
Sa		14. 15-20		9. 43b-50		27. 1-8
Pentecost 12						
M	Judg.	15. 1-8	Acts	27. 9-26	Luke	9. 51-62
Tu		15. 9-20		27. 27-44		10. 1-16
W		16. 1-22		28. 1-15		10. 17-24
T		16. 23-31		28. 16-31		10. 25-37
F		17	1 Cor.	1. 1-9		10. 38-42
Sa		18. 1-20, 27-31		1. 10-25		11. 1-13
Pentecost 13						
M	Ruth	1. 1-14	1 Cor.	1. 26 – 2. 5	Luke	11. 14-20
Tu		1. 15-22		2. 6-16		11. 21-28
W		2. 1-13		3. 1-9		11. 29-36
T		2. 14-23		3. 10-23		11. 37-44
F		3		4. 1-13		11. 45-54
Sa		4. 1-17		4. 14-21		12. 1-12
Pentecost 14						
M	Joel	1. 1-13	1 Cor.	5	Luke	12. 13-21
Tu		1. 14-20		6. 1-11		12. 22-31
W		2. 1-11		6. 12-20		12. 32-40
T		2. 12-22		7. 1-24		12. 41-48
F		2. 23-32		7. 25-40		12. 49-59
Sa		3. 9-21		8		13. 1-9

	Lesson (a)		Lesson (b)		Lesson (c)	
Pentecost 15						
M	Nah.	1. 1-10	1 Cor.	9. 1-14	Luke	13. 10-21
Tu		2. 1, 3-12		9. 15-27		13. 22-35
W		3. 1-3, 12-19		10. 1-13		14. 1-11
T	Hab.	1. 5-14		10. 14 – 11. 1		14. 12-24
F		2. 1-19		11. 2-22		14. 25-35
Sa		3		11. 23-34		15. 1-10
Pentecost 16						
M	Job	1. 1-12	1 Cor.	12. 1-11	Luke	15. 11-32
Tu		1. 13-22		12. 12-31		16. 1-18
W		2		13		16. 19-31
T		3. 1-17		14. 1-12		17. 1-10
F		4. 1-17		14. 13-25		17. 11-19
Sa		6. 1-13		14. 26-40		17. 20-37
Pentecost 17						
M	Job	13. 1-15	1 Cor.	15. 1-11	Luke	18. 1-14
Tu		14. 1-14		15. 12-19		18. 15-30
W		19. 14-27		15. 20-34		18. 31-43
T		28. 1-11		15. 35-49		19. 1-10
F		28. 12-28		15. 50-58		19. 11-27
Sa		31. 13-37	2 Cor.	1. 1-14		19. 28-40
Pentecost 18						
M	Job	38. 1-21	2 Cor.	1. 15 – 2. 4	Luke	19. 41-48
Tu		38. 22-41		2. 5-17		20. 1-8
W		39		3		20. 9-26
T		40		4		20. 27-40
F		41		5		20. 41 – 21. 4
Sa		42		6. 1-13		22. 1-13

	Lesson (a)		Lesson (b)	Lesson (c)
Pentecost 19				
M	Eccles. 1		2 Cor. 6. 14 – 7. 1	Luke 22. 14-23
Tu	3. 1-15		7. 2-16	22. 24-34
W	5. 1-12		8. 1-15	22. 35-46
T	7. 1-14		8. 16 – 9. 5	22. 47-62
F	9. 1-16		9. 6-15	22. 63-71
Sa	11. 9 – 12. 13		10	23. 1-12
Pentecost 20				
	Wisd. *or*	1 Chron.	2 Cor.	Luke
M	1	28. 1-10	11. 1-15	23. 13-25
Tu	2. 1-20	28. 11-21	11. 16-31	23. 26-43
W	2. 21 – 3. 9	29. 1-9	12	23. 44-56a
T	4. 7-17	29. 10-19	13	23. 56b –
			Jude	24. 12
F	6. 1-21	29. 20-30	1-16	24. 13-35
		2 Chron.		
Sa	7. 15 – 8. 1	1. 1-6	17-25	24. 36-53
Pentecost 21				
	Wisd. *or*	Song of Sol.	Eph.	Matt.
M	9	1. 9 – 2. 7	1. 1-14	5. 1-16
Tu	10.15–11.10	2. 8-17	1.15-23	5. 17-30
W	11.21–12.2	3	2. 1-10	5. 33-48
T	12. 12-21	5. 2 – 6. 3	2. 11-22	7. 1-11
	Baruch			
F	3. 1-14	7. 10 – 8. 4	3. 1-13	7. 12-20
Sa	4. 36 – 5. 9	8. 5-7	3. 14-21	7. 21-29

SECOND YEAR

		Lesson (a)		Lesson (b)		Lesson (c)
9 before Christmas						
M	Gen.	37. 1-11	Rom.	1. 1-17	Mark	1. 1-13
Tu		37. 12-24		1. 18-32		1. 14-20
W		37. 25-36		2. 1-16		1. 21-28
T		39. 1-6a		2. 17-29		1. 29-39
F		39. 6b-23		3. 1-20		1. 40-45
Sa		40		3. 21-31		2. 1-12
8 before Christmas						
M	Gen.	41. 1-13	Rom.	4. 1-12	Mark	2. 13-17
Tu		41. 14-45		4. 13-25		2. 18-22
W		41. 46-57		5. 1-11		2. 23-28
T		42. 1-17		5. 12-21		3. 1-6
F		42. 18-28		6. 1-14		3. 7-19a
Sa		42. 29-38		6. 15-23		3. 19b-30
7 before Christmas						
M	Gen.	43. 1-15	Rom.	7. 1-12	Mark	3. 31-35
Tu		43. 16-34		7. 13-25		4. 1-20
W		44. 1-17		8. 1-11		4. 21-34
T		44. 18-34		8. 12-17		4. 35-41
F		45. 1-15		8. 18-30		5. 1-20
Sa		45. 16-28		8. 31-39		5. 21-34
6 before Christmas						
M	Gen.	46. 1-7, 28-34	Rom.	9. 1-13	Mark	5. 35-43
Tu		47. 1-26		9. 14-29		6. 1-6
W		47. 27 – 48. 9		9. 30 – 10. 4		6. 7-13
T		48. 10-22		10. 5-13		6. 14-29
F		49. 29 – 50. 14		10. 14-21		6. 30-44
Sa		50. 15-26		11. 1-12		6. 45-56

	Lesson (a)	Lesson (b)	Lesson (c)

5 before Christmas

	Lesson (a)	Lesson (b)	Lesson (c)
M	Isa. 9. 8-17	Rom. 11. 13-24	Mark 7. 1-13
Tu	9. 18 – 10. 4	11. 25-36	7. 14-23
W	10. 5-19	12. 1-8	7. 24-30
T	10. 20-27	12. 9-21	7. 31-37
F	11. 10-16	13. 1-7	8. 1-10
Sa	12	13. 8-14	8. 11-21

4 before Christmas (Advent 1)

	Lesson (a)	Lesson (b)	Lesson (c)
M	Isa. 13. 1-13	Luke 17. 20-37	Rom. 14. 1-12
Tu	14. 3-15	19. 11-27	14. 13-23
W	15. 1 – 16. 5	19. 28-40	15. 1-6
T	19	19. 41-48	15. 7-13
F	24	20. 9-18	15. 14-22
Sa	26. 1-19	20. 19-26	15. 23-33

3 before Christmas (Advent 2)

	Lesson (a)	Lesson (b)	Lesson (c)
M	Dan. 7. 1-14	Luke 20. 27-40	1 Thess. 1
Tu	7. 15-27	20. 41 – 21. 4	2. 1-12
W	Zeph. 3. 11-20	21. 5-9	2. 13-20
T	Zech. 9. 9-12	21. 10-19	3
F	13	21. 20-28	4. 1-12
Sa	14. 1-9	21. 29-36	4. 13-18

2 before Christmas (Advent 3)

	Lesson (a)	Lesson (b)	Lesson (c)
M	Mal. 2. 17 – 3. 6	Matt. 3. 1-12	5. 1-11
Tu	4	Luke 7. 18-23	5. 12-28
W	1 Kgs. 21. 1-16	7. 24-28	2 Thess. 1
T	21. 17-29	7. 29-35	2. 1-12
F	Isa. 40. 3-8	Matt. 7. 13-21	2. 13-17
Sa	40. 9-11	7. 22-27	3

These are John Baptist passages.
Readings for 18-31 Dec. will take priority.

	Lesson (a)		Lesson (b)		Lesson (c)	
Weekdays						
18-31 December						
18	Isa.	55. 1-5	Phil.	2. 5-11	John	1. 15-28
19		55. 6-13		4. 4-9		1. 29-37
20		56. 1-5	Titus	2.11-15		3. 22-30
21		57. 15-21		3. 4-7		3. 31-36
22		58. 6-12	Rom.	1. 1-6		5. 39-47
23		59. 1-15a	Gal.	4. 1-7		7. 37-44
24		59. 15b-21	Eph.	3. 14-21		13. 1-17
Christmas Day		65. 17-25	1 John	1	John	3. 16-21
26		42. 1-9		2. 1-11		16. 31 – 17. 5
27		49. 1-6		2. 12-17		19. 25-27
28		50. 4-11		3. 1-10		15. 11-25
29		52. 13 – 53. 6		4. 17-21		12. 1-11
30		53. 7-12		5. 1-12		12. 20-33
31		51. 1-11		5. 13-21		12. 34-50

Christmas 1						
M	Isa.	60. 1-14	Luke	3. 1-14	1 Cor.	1. 1-9
Tu		60. 15-22		3. 15-22		1. 10-25
W		61. 1-7		4. 1-13		1. 26 – 2. 5
T		61. 8-11		4. 14-30		2. 6-16
F		62. 1-5		4. 31-44		3. 1-9
Sa		62. 6-12		5. 1-11		3. 10-23

Readings for 18-31 December will take priority.

	Lesson (a)		Lesson (b)		Lesson (c)	
Christmas 2						
M	Isa.	63. 1-6	Luke	5. 12-26	1 Cor.	4. 1-13
Tu		63. 7-14		5. 27-39		4. 14-21
W		63. 15 – 64. 5a		6. 1-11		5
T		64. 5b-12		6. 12-26		6. 1-11
F		65. 1-16		6. 27-38		6. 12-20
Sa		66. 1-2		6. 39-49		7. 1-24
Christmas 3						
M	Amos	1. 1-5	Luke	7. 1-10	1 Cor.	7. 25-40
Tu		2. 1-5		7. 11-23		8
W		2. 6-16		7. 24-35		9. 1-14
T		3. 1-8		7. 36-50		9. 15-27
F		4. 4-13		8. 1-15		10. 1-13
Sa		5. 1-15		8. 16-25		10. 14 – 11. 1
Christmas 4						
M	Amos	5. 16-24	Luke	8. 26-39	1 Cor.	11. 2-22
Tu		6. 1-8		8. 40-56		11. 23-34
W		7. 1-9		9. 1-9		12. 1-11
T		7. 10-17		9. 10-17		12. 12-31
F		8. 1-12		9. 18-27		13
Sa		9. 8-15		9. 28-43a		14. 1-12
Christmas 5						
M	Hos.	1. 1 – 2. 1	Luke	9. 43b-50	1 Cor.	14. 13-25
Tu		2. 2-15		9. 51-62		14. 26-40
W		2. 18 – 3. 5		10. 1-16		15. 1-19
T		6. 1-6		10. 17-24		15. 20-34
F		11. 1-9		10. 25-42		15. 35-49
Sa		14		11. 1-13		15. 50-58

	Lesson (a)	Lesson (b)	Lesson (c)
Christmas 6			
M	Mic. 1. 1-9	Luke 11. 14-28	2 Pet. 1. 1-11
Tu	2. 1-4, 12-13	11. 29-44	1. 12-21
W	3	11. 45-54	2. 1-10a
T	4. 1-5	12. 1-12	2. 10b-22
F	4. 8 – 5. 2	12. 13-34	3. 1-10
Sa	6. 1-8	12. 35-48	3. 11-18
9 before Easter			
M	1 Sam. 1. 1-20	2 Cor. 1. 1-14	Luke 12. 49-59
Tu	1. 21 – 2. 11	1. 15 – 2. 4	13. 1-17
W	3. 1-19	2. 5-17	13. 18-35
T	4. 1-18	3	14. 1-11
F	5	4	14. 12-24
Sa	6. 1-16	5	14. 25-35
8 before Easter			
M	1 Sam. 9. 1-14	2 Cor. 6. 1-11	Luke 15. 1-10
Tu	9. 15 – 10. 1	6. 12-18	15. 11-32
W	14. 1-15	7	16. 1-18
T	14. 24-46	8. 1-15	16. 19-31
F	15. 1-11	8. 16 – 9. 5	17. 1-19
Sa	15. 12-23	9. 6-15	17. 20-37
7 before Easter			
M	1 Sam. 16. 1-13	2 Cor. 10	Luke 18. 1-14
Tu	16. 14-23	11. 1-15	18. 15-30
Ash Wed	Joel 2. 12-17	1 Cor. 9. 19-27	Matt. 6. 16-21
T	1 Sam. 17. 1-25	2 Cor. 11. 16-33	Luke 18. 31-43
F	17. 26-50	12	22. 1-23
Sa	18. 1-16	13	22. 24-38

	Lesson (a)		Lesson (b)		Lesson (c)
6 before Easter (Lent 1)					
M	1 Sam. 19. 1-18	Gal.	1. 1-10	Luke	22. 39-53
Tu	20. 1-23		1. 11-24		22. 54-71
W	20. 24-42		2. 1-10		23. 1-12
T	24		2. 11-21		23. 13-31
F	31		3. 1-14		23. 32-43
Sa	2 Sam. 1		3. 15-22		23. 44-56a
5 before Easter (Lent 2)					
M	2 Sam. 2. 1-11	Mark	9. 2-13	Gal.	3. 23-29
Tu	5. 1-10, 17-25		9. 14-29		4. 1-11
W	6. 1-19		9. 30-50		4. 12-20
T	7. 1-13		10. 1-12		4. 21 – 5. 1
F	7. 18-29		10. 13-22		5. 2-12
Sa	9		10. 23-31		5. 13-25
4 before Easter (Lent 3)					
M	2 Sam. 11. 1-17	Mark	10. 32-45	Gal.	6. 1-10
Tu	11. 18-27		10. 46-52		6. 11-18
W	12. 1-14		11. 1-11	Col.	1. 1-14
T	12. 15-25		11. 12-19		1. 15-29
F	15. 1-15		11. 20-26		2. 1-15
Sa	15. 16-37		11. 27-33		2. 16 – 3. 11
3 before Easter (Lent 4)					
M	2 Sam. 16. 1-14	Mark	12. 1-12	Col.	3. 12-25
Tu	17. 1-14		12. 13-27		4
W	17. 15-23		12. 28-44	Jas.	1. 1-11
T	18. 1-18		13. 1-13		1. 12-18
F	18. 19-33		13. 14-27		1. 19-27
Sa	19. 1-15		13. 28-37		2. 1-13

	Lesson (a)		Lesson (b)		Lesson (c)	
2 before Easter (Passion Sunday)						
M	2 Sam.	19. 16-30	Mark	14. 1-11	Jas.	2. 14-26
Tu		19. 31-43		14. 12-31		3. 1-12
W		23. 1-7		14. 32-52		3. 13-18
T		23. 8-23		14. 53-65		4. 1-12
F		24. 1-14		14. 66-72		4. 13 – 5. 6
Sa		24. 15-25		15. 1-20		5. 7-20
1 before Easter (Palm Sunday)						
Holy Week						
M	Isa.	5. 1-7	John	16. 1-15	Heb.	2. 9-18
Tu	Wisd.	1.1, 12-16		16. 16-33		8. 1-6
	or Jer.	11. 18-20				
W	Isa.	63. 1-9		17. 1-18		9. 11-15
T	Exod.	13. 3-10		17. 19-26		9. 16-28
Good Fri	Gen.	22. 1-18	Matt.	27. 27-56 *or*		10. 1-10
			John	18. 1 – 19. 37		
Sa	Job	19. 21-27		19. 38-42	1 Pet.	4. 1-6
Easter Week						
M	Exod.	15. 1-12	John	20. 1-10	Eph.	1. 1-14
Tu		15. 13-21		20. 11-23		1. 15-23
W	Isa.	25. 1-9		20. 24-31		2. 1-10
T	Jer.	31. 1-14		21. 1-14		2. 11-22
F	Job	14. 1-14		21. 15-19		3. 1-13
Sa	Mic.	7. 7-20		21. 20-25		3. 14-21
Easter 1						
M	1 Kgs.	1. 5-31	Eph.	4. 1-16	John	1. 1-18
Tu		1. 38-53		4. 17-32		1. 19-34
W		2. 1-12		5. 1-14		1. 35-51
T		3. 3-15		5. 15-33		2. 1-12
F		5. 1-12		6. 1-9		2. 13-25
Sa		6. 1-14		6. 10-24		3. 1-15

		Lesson (a)		Lesson (b)		Lesson (c)
Easter 2						
M	1 Kgs.	8. 1-21	Rev.	1. 1-8	John	3. 16-21
Tu		11. 1-13		1. 9-20		3. 22-36
W		11. 26-40		2. 1-11		4. 1-26
T		11. 43 – 12. 16		2. 12-17		4. 27-42
F		12. 25-33		2. 18-29		4. 43-54
Sa		13. 1-10		3. 1-6		5. 1-18
Easter 3						
M	1 Kgs.	20. 1-21	Rev.	3. 7-13	John	5. 19-29
Tu		20. 22-43		3. 14-22		5. 30-40
W		21. 1-16		4		5. 41-47
T		21. 17-29		5		6. 1-15
F		22. 1-28		6		6. 16-29
Sa		22. 29-40		7. 1-8		6. 30-40
Easter 4						
M	2 Kgs.	2. 1-15	Rev.	7. 9-17	John	6. 41-51
Tu		3. 4-24		11. 1-13		6. 52-59
W		4. 1-17		11. 14-19		6. 60-71
T		5. 1-19a		12. 1-6		7. 1-13
F		5. 19b-27		12. 7-17		7. 14-24
Sa		6. 8-23		13. 1-10		7. 25-36
Easter 5						
M	2 Kgs.	6. 24 – 7. 2	Rev.	13. 11-18	John	7. 37-52
Tu		7. 3-20		14. 1-13		8. 12-20
W		9. 1-13		14. 14-20		8. 21-30
Ascension Day	Song of 3 Ch.	29-37 *or*	Heb.	9. 19-28	Mark	16. 14-20
	Ezek.	1. 4-5, 26-8				
F	2 Kgs.	9. 14-37	Rev.	19. 1-10	John	8. 31-47
Sa		10. 18-28		19. 11-16 (*or* -21)		8. 48-59

		Lesson (a)		Lesson (b)		Lesson (c)
Easter 6						
M	2 Kgs.	17. 1-14	Rev.	20	John	9. 1-12
Tu		18. 1-12		21. 1-8		9. 13-23
W		18. 13-25		21. 9-21		9. 24-41
T		19. 1-19		21. 22 – 22. 5		10. 1-16
F		19. 20-37		22. 6-13		10. 17-30
Sa		20. 1-20		22. 14-21		10. 31-42
Pentecost						
M	Num.	27. 12-23	Luke	1. 26-38	Phil.	1. 1-8
Tu	2 Sam.	23. 1-5		2. 22-32		1. 9-18
W	Ezek.	36. 22-28		3. 15-22		1. 19-26
T	Zech.	4. 1-10		4. 16-21		1. 27 – 2. 4
F	Isa.	44. 1-8		11. 5-13		2. 5-18
Sa	Ezek.	37. 1-14		12. 8-12		2. 19-30
Pentecost 1						
M	2 Kgs.	22. 3-20	John	11. 1-16	Phil.	3. 1-11
Tu		23. 1-10		11. 17-37		3. 12 – 4. 1
W		23. 21-30		11. 38-45		4. 2-9
T		24. 8-17		11. 46-57		4. 10-20
F		24. 18 – 25. 12		12. 1-11	1 Tim.	1. 1-17
Sa		25. 22-30		12. 12-19		1. 18 – 2. 15
Pentecost 2						
M	Ezek.	1. 1-14	John	12. 20-36a	1 Tim.	3
Tu		1. 15 – 2. 2		12. 36b-50		4
W		2. 3 – 3. 11		13. 1-11		5. 1-16
T		3. 12-27		13. 12-20		5. 17-25
F		5. 5-12		13. 21-30		6. 1-10
Sa		8. 1-12		13. 31-38		6. 11-21

	Lesson (a)	Lesson (b)	Lesson (c)
Pentecost 3			
M	Ezek. 9	John 14. 1-11	2 Tim. 1. 1-14
Tu	10. 1-19	14. 12-31	1. 15 – 2. 13
W	11. 14-25	15. 1-17	2. 14-26
T	14. 12-23	15. 18-27	3
F	18	16. 1-15	4. 1-18
Sa	24. 15-27	16. 16-33	Titus 1
Pentecost 4			
M	Ezek. 26. 1-14	John 17. 1-11	Titus 2
Tu	28. 1-10	17. 12-18	3
W	32. 17-32	17. 19-26	Philemon
T	33. 1-9	18. 1-11	Heb. 1
F	33. 10-20	18. 12-18, 25-27	2. 1-9
Sa	33. 21-33	18. 19-24	2. 10-18
Pentecost 5			
M	Ezek. 34. 1-10	John 18. 28-40	Heb. 3
Tu	34. 11-16	19. 1-16a	4. 1-10
W	34. 17-31	19. 16b-24	4. 11-16
T	36. 1-15	19. 25-30	5
F	36. 16-32	19. 31-37	6. 1-12
Sa	36. 33-38	19. 38-42	6. 13-20
Pentecost 6			
M	Ezek. 37. 15-28	John 20. 1-10	Heb. 7. 1-10
Tu	38. 10-23	20. 11-23	7. 11-28
W	39. 21-29	20. 24-31	8
T	43. 1-9	21. 1-14	9. 1-14
F	44. 4-8	21. 15-19	9. 15-28
Sa	47. 1-12	21. 20-25	10. 1-18

		Lesson (a)		Lesson (b)		Lesson (c)
Pentecost 7						
M	Dan.	1	Heb.	10. 19-39	Matt.	1. 18-25
Tu		2. 1-12		11. 1-12		2
W		2. 13-24		11. 13-22		3
T		2. 25-46		11. 23-40		4. 1-11
F		3. 1-18		12. 1-11		4. 12-25
Sa		3. 19-30		12. 12-29		5. 1-12
Pentecost 8						
M	Dan.	4. 1-18	Heb.	13. 1-6	Matt.	5. 13-20
Tu		4. 19-37		13. 7-16		5. 21-26
W		5. 1-12		13. 17-25		5. 27-37
T		5. 13-30	1 Pet.	1. 1-12		5. 38-48
F		6. 1-14		1. 13-25		6. 1-15
Sa		6. 15-28		2. 1-10		6. 16-34
Pentecost 9						
M	Dan.	8. 1-14	1 Pet.	2. 11-25	Matt.	7. 1-12
Tu		8. 15-27		3. 1-12		7. 13-29
W		9. 1-19		3. 13-22		8. 1-13
T		9. 20-27		4. 1-11		8. 14-22
F		10. 1-14		4. 12-19		8. 23-34
Sa		12		5		9. 1-8
Pentecost 10						
M	Ezra	1	Acts	1. 1-14	Matt.	9. 9-17
Tu		3		1. 15-26		9. 18-26
W		7. 11-28		2. 1-13		9. 27-38
T		8. 15-32		2. 14-36		10. 1-8
F	Neh.	1		2. 37-47		10. 9-15
Sa		2		3. 1-10		10. 16-23

		Lesson (a)		Lesson (b)		Lesson (c)
Pentecost 11						
M	Neh.	4. 1-14	Acts	3. 11 – 4. 4	Matt.	10. 24-33
Tu		4. 15-23		4. 5-22		10. 34 – 11. 1
W		6. 1-15		4. 23-31		11. 2-6
T		8. 1-12		4. 32 – 5. 11		11. 7-19
F		8. 13-18		5. 12-26		11. 20-30
Sa		13. 15-22		5. 27-42		12. 1-8
Pentecost 12						
M	Jonah	1. 1-16	Matt.	12. 9-21	Acts	6
Tu		1. 17 – 2. 10		12. 22-37		7. 1-16
W		3		12. 38-50		7. 17-36
T		4		13. 1-9		7. 37-53
F	Hag.	1. 1-11		13. 10-23		7. 54 – 8. 3
Sa		1. 12 – 2. 9		13. 24-33		8. 4-25
Pentecost 13						
M	Zech.	1. 7-17	Matt.	13. 34-43	Acts	8. 26-40
Tu		1. 18 – 2. 13		13. 44-58		9. 1-19a
W		3		14. 1-12		9. 19b-31
T		4		14. 13-21		9. 32-43
F		5		14. 22-36		10. 1-16
Sa		6. 1-8		15. 1-20		10. 17-33
Pentecost 14						
M	Zech.	6. 9-15	Matt.	15. 21-28	Acts	10. 34-48
Tu		7. 1-7		15. 29-39		11. 1-18
W		7. 8-14		16. 1-12		11. 19-30
T		8. 1-8		16. 13-28		12. 1-11
F		8. 9-17		17. 1-13		12. 12-25
Sa		8. 18-23		17. 14-27		13. 1-12

		Lesson (a)		Lesson (b)		Lesson (c)
Pentecost 15						
M	Prov.	1. 20-33	Matt.	18. 1-10	Acts	13. 13-41
Tu		3. 11-20		18. 11-22		13. 42 – 14. 7
W		4		18. 23-35		14. 8-23
T		6. 6-19		19. 1-15		15. 1-21
F		7. 6-23		19. 16-23		15. 22-35
Sa		8. 1-21		19. 24-30		15. 36 – 16. 5
Pentecost 16						
M	Prov.	8. 22-36	Matt.	20. 1-16	Acts	16. 6-24
Tu		9. 1-10		20. 17-34		16. 25-40
W		10. 1-13		21. 1-17		17. 1-15
T		11. 1-12		21. 18-32		17. 16-34
F		12. 9-22		21. 33-46		18. 1-21
Sa		13. 7-25		22. 1-14		18. 22 – 19. 7
Pentecost 17						
M	Prov.	14. 1-12	Matt.	22. 15-33	Acts	19. 8-20
Tu		14. 27-35		22. 34-46		19. 21-41
W		15. 1-15		23. 1-12		20. 1-16
T		15. 16-33		23. 13-39		20. 17-38
F		16. 16-32		24. 1-14		21. 1-16
Sa		18. 9-24		24. 15-28		21. 17-26

Pentecost 18

	Prov. *or*	Ecclus.	Acts	Matt.
M	22. 1-12	2	21. 27-39	24. 29-34
Tu	23. 15-25	4. 11-28	21. 40 – 22. 21	24. 35-51
W	24. 19-34	4. 29 – 6. 1	22. 22 – 23. 11	25. 1-13
T	25. 11-28	11. 7-28	23. 12-35	25. 14-30
F	26. 1-12	18. 1-13	24. 1-23	25. 31-46
Sa	27. 6-22	28. 1-12	24. 24 – 25. 12	26. 1-13

	Lesson (a)		Lesson (b)		Lesson (c)	
Pentecost 19						
	Prov. *or*	Ecclus.				
M	28. 12-28	29. 1-13	Acts	25. 13-27	Matt.	26. 14-29
Tu	29. 11-27	35. 1-11		26. 1-23		26. 30-46
W	30. 1-9	36. 1-17		26. 24-32		26. 47-56
T	30. 15-31	44. 1-15		27. 1-8		26. 57-75
F	31. 10-31	51. 1-12		27. 9-26		27. 1-10
Sa	Obadiah	51. 13-30		27. 27-44		27. 11-26
Pentecost 20						
	Esther *or*	1 Macc.				
M	2. 5-18	1. 1-15	Acts	28. 1-15	Matt.	27. 27-37
Tu	2.20–3.6	1. 16-40		28. 16-31		27. 38-44
W	3.7–4.3	1. 41-64	Jude	1-16		27. 45-56
T	4.4–5.14	2. 1-22		17-25		27. 57-66
F	6.1–7.10	2. 23-48	2 John			28. 1-10
Sa	8	2. 49-69	3 John			28. 11-20
Pentecost 21						
	Lev. *or*	1 Macc.				
M	23. 1-22	3. 1-26	Eph.	4. 1-16	Luke	6. 20-26
Tu	23. 23-44	3. 42-60		4. 17-32		6. 27-38
W	25. 1-24	4. 1-25		5. 1-14		6. 39-49
T	25. 25-55	4. 36-51		5. 15-33	Matt.	6. 1-13
F	26. 1-13	4. 52-61		6. 1-9		6. 14-23
Sa	26. 14-20, 38-45	Pr. of Manasses		6. 10-24		6. 24-34

CANTICLES

SEASONAL

Advent

DEUTERONOMY 32. 1–12

You heavens, listen to my voice:
earth, hear the words I speak.
My teaching will fall like the rain:
my words drop down like dew;
like showers on the fresh grass:
like rain on the tender shoots.

While I tell of the Lord's renown:
proclaim the greatness of our God.
He is the rock: his deeds are perfect
and all his ways are just;
God who is perfect and true:
God who is holy and just.

O crooked and perverse generation,
how can you be his children?
Is this how you repay the Lord,
you foolish and stupid people!

Is he not your father who fashioned you?
Did he not make you and give you life?
Remember the days of old.
Remember the days long ago.
Ask your father and he will tell you:
Ask the elders and they will teach you.

When the Most High divided the nations
and dispersed the sons of men,
he fixed the boundaries of the nations
according to the number of his children.
But the Lord's share was on his own people:
Jacob was his allotted portion.

He adopted them when they were in the desert
in the waste and howling wilderness.
He protected them and kept them safe
as the apple of his eye.
Like an eagle protecting his nest,
watching over his brood,
he spread out his wings to guard them
and supported them on his pinions.

The Lord alone was their guide,
no other god but he.

1 SAMUEL 2. 1-10

My heart exults in the Lord,
in my God I lift high my head.
My mouth derides my foes,
for I rejoice in your saving power.
There is no god except the Lord:
there is none so holy as he.
No stronghold can compare with God.

Cease then your vain boasting;
let no arrogance pass your lips;
for the Lord God is all-knowing:
he appraises the deeds of men.

The bow of the mighty is broken,
but the weak are girded with strength.
The rich sell themselves for a crust,
but the hungry rest from their toil.
The barren woman has seven children,
but the fruitful mother is deserted.

It is the Lord who gives life and death:
sends to Sheol, and raises to life;
the Lord makes the rich and the poor,
he humbles and likewise exalts.

He raises the poor from the dust,
from the dunghill he raises the lowly,

to give them a place with princes
and set them in seats of honour.
For the foundations of the earth are the Lord's:
on them he has poised the world.

He guides the steps of the faithful,
while the wicked vanish in darkness:
no human strength can avail them.
The foes of the Lord are routed
when the Most High thunders from heaven.
The Lord is judge of the world:
he endows the king with strength,
raises high the head of his Anointed.

Isaiah 2. 2–5

In days to come
the mountain where the Lord dwells
will be lifted high above all the mountains
and raised above the hills.
All the nations will flock to it:
countless peoples will come to it.

And they will say:
'Come, let us go to the mountain of the Lord,
to the Temple of the God of Jacob.
He will teach us his ways
and we will walk in his paths.'
For the Law will go out from Zion,
the word of the Lord from Jerusalem.
He will sit in judgement over the nations:
be arbiter among many peoples.
They will beat their swords into ploughshares,
and their spears into sickles;
nation shall not lift sword against nation,
nor ever again prepare for war.

O people of Jacob, come:
let us walk in the light of the Lord.

REVELATION 19. 1,2,5-7

Alleluia!
Victory, glory, and power to our God,
for right and just are his judgements.
Praise our God, all you who serve him,
you who fear him, great and small.

Alleluia!
The Lord our God Almighty has claimed his kingdom.
Let us rejoice and triumph and give him praise:
the time has come for the wedding-feast of the Lamb.

Christmas

EPHESIANS 1. 3-10

Blessed be God the Father of our Lord Jesus Christ,
who has bestowed on us all the spiritual blessings of heaven.
In Christ he chose us before the world was made,
to be holy without blemish,
and to live by love in his presence.

He destined us by his decree
to be his adopted sons through Jesus Christ,
that we might praise the glory of his grace,
his free gift to us in the Beloved.
In him we gain redemption,
our sins forgiven by the shedding of his blood.

Such is the richness of his grace,
which he has lavished on us
in all wisdom and discernment.

He has revealed to us the mystery of his plan,
hidden in Christ from the beginning
and put into effect when the time was ripe:
to bring everything in heaven and on earth
under the headship of Christ.

Epiphany

ISAIAH 40. 9–11

Herald of joyful news to Zion,
take your stand upon the height:
lift up your voice and cry aloud,
you who bring Jerusalem good news.
Shout without fear to the town of Judah:
'Here is your God.'

Here is the Lord coming in power,
coming to rule with his mighty arm.
With him come his spoils:
his trophies go before him.

He will tend his flock like a shepherd,
gathering his lambs in his arm,
holding them to his breast,
and leading the ewes to water.

Passiontide

PHILIPPIANS 2. 6–11

Let this mind be in you which was in Christ Jesus:
the divine nature was his from the first,
yet he did not grasp at equality with God.
He emptied himself and became like a slave.

Taking the nature of man,
he was revealed in human form.
He humbled himself and became obedient even to death,
death on a cross.

Therefore God has raised him on high
and given him a name above every other name:
so that in the name of Jesus every knee shall bow—
in heaven, on earth, and in the depths—
and every tongue confess that Jesus Christ is Lord,
to the glory of God the Father.

1 PETER 2. 21-24

Christ suffered for your sake
and left an example for you to follow.
He did no wrong, no deceit was found on his lips.
He was insulted, but offered no insult in return.
He suffered, and threatened no vengeance,
but committed his cause to the One who judges justly.
On the cross he bore our sins in his own body,
so that we might die to sin and live in holiness.
By his wounds you have been healed.

You were straying like sheep,
but now you have come back
to the shepherd and guardian of your souls.

Easter Vigil (Baptism)

EXODUS 15. 1-4a, 8-13, 17-18

I sing to the Lord, so great and so glorious;
horse and rider he has hurled into the sea.
The Lord is my strength and my song:
the Lord himself is my saviour.
He is my God and I will praise him:
the God of my father, I exalt him.
The Lord is a warrior:
The Lord is his name.
Pharaoh's chariots and army he has hurled into the sea:
the Red Sea engulfs them, the pride of his horsemen.

At the blast of your anger the waters piled high:
the waves were still, the sea-bed grew firm.
'After them, seize them,' the enemy cried:
'There will be spoils for all, to your hearts' content.
I will draw my sword and destroy them.'

One breath from you, and the sea closed over them:
they sank like lead in the raging waters.

Who among the gods is your equal, Lord?
Who so majestic, so worthy of awe,
so worthy of praise for your mighty deeds?
You stretched out your hand, and the waters engulfed them.

Constant in love you have led your ransomed people;
by your strength you have guided them to your holy dwelling.

On your mountain you will settle them, Lord,
in the dwelling you have made your own,
the sanctuary your hands have prepared.
The Lord will be our king for ever and ever.

Isaiah 12. 1-6

On that day you will say:
I give thanks to you, Lord;
you were angry with me,
but your anger has ceased
and you have given me comfort.

He is indeed the God of my salvation.
I trust him and have no fear,
for the Lord is my strength and my song.
He is my salvation;
from the springs of salvation
you will draw water with joy.
On that day you will say:
Give thanks to the Lord,
call upon his name.

Make known his deeds among the people:
declare the greatness of his name.
Sing to the Lord for his marvellous deeds:
make them known to all the earth.
Cry out with joy and gladness,
all you who dwell in Zion:
for great in your midst
is the holy one of Israel.

·Isaiah 66. 10–14a

Lovers of Jerusalem, rejoice with her:
rejoice with her, all you who mourned her;
and you will be filled with her delights
like babes consoled at the breast.

For thus says the Lord:
The rivers of my peace will flow over her,
and the wealth of the nations, like a stream in spate.

This will be the milk you drink,
like children suckled at the breast,
and fondled in their mother's arms.
I will comfort you as a mother caresses her child:
your comfort will be in Jerusalem.
All this you will see and be glad
and your limbs will grow strong as the fresh grass.

Easter (see also Easter Vigil: Baptism)

Colossians 1. 12–20

Give thanks to the Father
who has enabled you to join the saints
and share the light they inherit.
He has taken us out of darkness
and placed us in the light of the kingdom of his beloved Son.
In him we find freedom and the forgiveness of our sins.

He is the image of the unseen God,
the first-born of all creation.
In him all things in heaven and earth were created,
all that we see, and all that remains unseen:
Thrones, Dominations, Sovereignties, and Powers—
all things were created through him and for him.

He exists before all creation:
in him all things subsist.
He too is the head of the Church, which is his body.
He is its origin, the first-born from the dead:
in every way the primacy is his.

For God decreed that all perfection should be found in him,
and all things in heaven and on earth should be reconciled in him,
who brought peace by his death on the cross.

Ascension

ISAIAH 42. 10–13

Sing a new hymn to the Lord:
Sing his praises from the end of the earth.

Praise him, all you who sail the seas,
and all you creatures who dwell within the sea.

Let the islands and their dwellers praise the Lord.
Let the desert and its townships raise their voice,
and those who dwell in the settlements of Kedar.

Cry aloud, you inhabitants of Sela.
Let your voices be heard from the hill-tops,
and from the islands proclaim the Lord's glory.

The Lord goes forth like a hero:
as a warrior, summoned to battle,
marches valiantly against his foe.

1 TIMOTHY 3. 16

Christ, who was made manifest in the body,
vindicated by the Spirit,
seen by angels,
proclaimed among the nations,
and believed in by the world,
has been taken up into glory.

Pentecost

I will pour out my Spirit on all flesh.
Your sons and daughters shall prophesy,
your old men shall dream dreams
and your young men shall see visions.

I will pray the Father
and he will give you another Counsellor
to be with you for ever.
When the Spirit of truth comes,
he will guide you into all the truth.

The Counsellor, the Holy Spirit
whom the Father will send in my name,
he will teach you all things,
and bring to remembrance
all that I have said to you.

And suddenly a sound came from heaven
like the rush of a mighty wind,
and it filled the whole house where they were sitting,
and they were all filled with the Holy Spirit.

Likewise the Spirit helps us in our weakness,
for we do not know how to pray as we ought,
but the Spirit himself intercedes for us
with sighs too deep for words. (9)

EZEKIEL 36. 24–28

I will take you from the nations
and gather you from every country
and bring you home to your own land.

And I will pour clean water over you,
purify you from all defilement,
and cleanse you from your idols.

I will give you a new heart
and put a new spirit within you;
I will take from your flesh the heart of stone
and give you a heart of flesh.

And I will put my spirit within you
and make you walk in my ways
and observe my decrees.

You will live in the land
that I gave to your fathers;
and you will be my people
and I will be your God.

GENERAL

A Song of David

1 CHRONICLES 29. 10–13

May you be blessed, Lord God of our father Israel:
from creation and for ever.

Yours is the greatness, Lord, and the power and glory, the splendour and the majesty:
for everything in heaven and earth is yours.

Yours is the sovereignty, Lord, and you are exalted as head above all:
from you come riches and honour, and you rule over all things.

In your hand lie strength and power:
and yours it is to give greatness and strength to all.

And now our God we give you thanks:
and praise the splendour of your name. (11)

Glory to the Father and to the Son:
and to the Holy Spirit;

as it was in the beginning, is now:
and shall be for ever. Amen.

We have a strong city

ISAIAH 26. 1-4, 7, 8

We have a strong city:
God has made salvation its walls and ramparts.

Open the gates to let a righteous nation in:
even a nation that is faithful.

You keep in peace the man whose mind is stayed on you:
in peace because he trusts in you.

Trust in the Lord for ever:
for the Lord himself is an everlasting rock.

The path of the upright is straight:
you who are the righteous God, mark out the right way for the just.

We too seek the path prescribed in your laws, O Lord:
your presence and your power are all our hearts' desire. (11)

Glory to the Father . . .

Christ the Servant

1 PETER 2. 21-24

Jesus Christ suffered for you, leaving you an example:
that you should follow in his steps.

He committed no sin, no guile was found on his lips:
when he was reviled he did not revile in return.

When he suffered he did not threaten:
but trusted in him who judges justly.

He himself bore our sins in his body on the tree:
that we might die to sin and live to righteousness.

By his wounds you have been healed:
for you were straying like sheep.

But now you have returned:
to the shepherd and guardian of your souls. (11)

Glory to the Father . . .

A Song of Love

1 JOHN 4. 7,8; 1 CORINTHIANS 13. 4-10,12,13

Christians, let us love one another:
because love comes from God.

He who loves is born of God and knows him:
but he who does not love does not know God.

Love does not insist on its own way, it is not quick to take offence:
it does not rejoice at wrong, but rejoices in the right.

Love is patient and kind:
love is not jealous or boastful, it is not arrogant or rude.

Love bears all things and believes all things:
love hopes and endures all things.

Love will never come to an end:
but prophecy will vanish, tongues cease, and knowledge pass away.

For our knowledge and our prophecy are both imperfect:
but when the perfect comes, the imperfect will pass away.

Now I know in part:
but then I shall understand fully, even as I have been fully understood.

There are three things that last for ever, faith, hope, and love:
but the greatest of these is love. (11)

Glory to the Father . . .

A Song of Assurance

ROMANS 8. 28-35, 37

God works for good in everything with those who love him:
who are called according to his purpose.

For those whom he foreknew:
he also predestined to be conformed to the image of his Son.

And those whom he predestined he also called:
and those whom he called he also justified.

And to those whom he justified:
he has also given his splendour.

If God is on our side:
who can ever be against us?

He who did not spare his own Son, but gave him up for us all:
will he not also with him freely give us all things?

It is God who justifies:
who then can ever condemn us?

For it is Christ Jesus who died and was raised from the dead:
who is at God's right hand to plead our cause.

What can separate us from the love of Christ:
can persecution or hunger, can peril or the sword?

No, in all these things we are more than conquerors:
through him who loved us, even Jesus Christ our Lord. (11)

Glory to the Father . . .

A Song of Salvation

ROMANS 5. 1-8; 8. 37-39

Now that we have been justified through faith:
we are at peace with God through Jesus Christ our Lord.

And so we exult in our hope of the splendour of God:
and we even exult in the sufferings we endure.

For our hope is not in vain:
because God's love has flooded our inmost hearts through the Holy Spirit.

When we were still powerless, Christ died for the wicked:
he died for us while we were still sinners, and so God proves his love toward us.

We are more than conquerors through him who loved us:
for nothing can separate us from God's love in Jesus Christ our Lord. (11)

Glory to the Father . . .

Psalm 19. 7-14

God's perfect law revives the soul,
His word makes wise the simple;
God's clear commands rejoice the heart,
His light the eye enlightens;
God's fear is pure, his judgements just,
More to be sought than pure fine gold,
Sweeter by far than honey.

Lord, who can tell the secret faults
That have dominion o'er me?
Hold back thy servant from self-will
And break its power to bind me.
May all I think and all I say
Be now acceptable to thee,
My Rock and my Redeemer. (12)

Psalm 51. 1-12

O God, be gracious to me in thy love,
And in thy mercy pardon my misdeeds;
Wash me from guilt and cleanse me from my sin,
For well I know the evil I have done.

Against thee, Lord, thee only have I sinned,
And what to thee is hateful have I done;
I own thy righteousness in charging me,
I know thee justified should'st thou condemn.

Take hyssop, sprinkle me and make me clean,
Wash me and make me whiter than the snow;
Fill me with gladness and rejoicing, Lord,
And let my broken frame know joy once more.

Turn thou thy face, O God, from my misdeeds,
And blot out all the sins that sully me;
Create a clean and contrite heart in me,
Renew my soul in faithfulness and love.

Drive me not from thy presence, gracious Lord,
Nor keep thy Holy Spirit far from me;
Restore my soul with thy salvation's joy,
And with a willing spirit strengthen me. (12)

Psalm 139

Thou art before me, Lord, thou art behind,
And thou above me hast spread out thy hand;
Such knowledge is too wonderful for me,
Too high to grasp, too great to understand.

Then whither from thy Spirit shall I go,
And whither from thy presence shall I flee?
If I ascend to heaven thou art there,
And in the lowest depths I meet with thee.

If I should take my flight into the dawn,
If I should dwell on ocean's farthest shore,
Thy mighty hand would rest upon me still,
And thy right hand would guard me evermore.

If I should say 'Darkness will cover me,
And I shall hide within the veil of night',
Surely the darkness is not dark to thee,
The night is as the day, the darkness light.

Search me, O God, search me and know my heart,
Try me, O God, my mind and my spirit try;
Keep me from any path that gives thee pain,
And lead me in the everlasting way. (12)

COLLECTS FOR THE DAILY OFFICE

9th before Christmas

Almighty God,
you have created the heavens and the earth
and made man in your own image.
Teach us to discern your hand in all your works
and to serve you with reverence and thanksgiving;
through Jesus Christ our Lord,
who with you and the Holy Spirit reigns supreme over all things
now and for ever.

8th before Christmas

1 Heavenly Father,
whose blessed Son was revealed
that he might destroy the works of the devil
and make us the sons of God
and heirs of eternal life:
grant that we, having this hope,
may purify ourselves even as he is pure;
that when he shall appear in power and great glory
we may be made like him in his eternal and glorious kingdom;
where he is alive and reigns with you and the Holy Spirit,
one God, now and for ever. (1)

2 Almighty God,
you have given your Son Jesus Christ
to break the power of evil.
Free us from all that darkens and ensnares us
and bring us to eternal light and joy;
through the power of him
who is alive and reigns with you and the Holy Spirit,
one God, now and for ever.

7th before Christmas

Almighty God,
whose chosen servant Abraham
faithfully obeyed your call
and rejoiced in your promise
that, in him, all the families of the earth should be blessed:
give us a faith like his,
that, in us, your promises may be fulfilled:
through Jesus Christ our Lord.

6th before Christmas

Lord God our redeemer,
who heard the cry of your people
and sent your servant Moses to lead them out of slavery;
free us from the tyranny of sin and death
and, by the leading of your Spirit,
bring us to our promised land;
through Jesus Christ our Lord. (13b)

5th before Christmas

Almighty God,
you spoke to the prophets
and put your word on their lips,
that they might make your will and purpose known.
Speak to us now
and make us ready to hear and answer your call;
through Jesus Christ our Lord.

4th before Christmas

Almighty God,
give us grace to cast away the works of darkness
and to put on the armour of light,
now in the time of this mortal life,
in which your Son Jesus Christ came to us in great humility:
so that on the last day,
when he shall come again in his glorious majesty
to judge the living and the dead,
we may rise to the life immortal:
through him who is alive and reigns with you and the Holy Spirit,
now and for ever. (1)

3rd before Christmas

Blessed Lord,
who caused all holy Scriptures to be written for our learning:
help us so to hear them,
to read, mark, learn, and inwardly digest them
that, through patience, and the comfort of your holy word,
we may embrace and for ever hold fast
the hope of everlasting life,
which you have given us in our Saviour Jesus Christ. (1)

2nd before Christmas

Almighty God,
who sent your servant John the Baptist
to prepare your people for the coming of your Son:
inspire the ministers and stewards of your truth
to turn our disobedient hearts to the law of love;
that when he comes again in glory
we may stand with confidence before him as our judge;
who is alive and reigns with you and the Holy Spirit,
one God, now and for ever.

1st before Christmas

Heavenly Father,
who chose the Virgin Mary, full of grace,
to be the mother of our Lord and Saviour:
fill us with your grace,
that in all things we may accept your holy will
and with her rejoice in your salvation;
through Jesus Christ our Lord. (14)

Christmas Day

1 Eternal God,
who made this most holy night
to shine with the brightness of your one true light:
bring us who have known the revelation of that light on earth,
to see the radiance of your heavenly glory;
through Jesus Christ our Lord.

2 Almighty God
who wonderfully created us in your image
and yet more wonderfully restored us
through your Son Jesus Christ:
grant that, as he came to share in our humanity,
so may we share in the life of his divinity;
who is alive and reigns with you and the Holy Spirit,
one God, now and for ever.

3 All praise to you, Almighty God and heavenly king,
who sent your Son into the world
to take our nature upon him
and to be born of a pure virgin:
grant that, as we are born again in him,
so he may continually dwell in us
and reign on earth as he reigns in heaven
with you and the Holy Spirit
now and for ever.

Christmas 1

Eternal God,
who by the shining of a star
led the wise men to the worship of your Son:
guide by his light the nations of the earth,
that the whole world may behold your glory;
through Jesus Christ our Lord.

Christmas 2

Heavenly Father,
your only Son came into the world to do your will.
Grant that with the pattern of his life before our eyes
we may delight to work with him
  for the coming of your kingdom;
through Jesus Christ our Lord. (15)

Christmas 3

Almighty God,
who anointed Jesus at his baptism with the Holy Spirit
and revealed him as your beloved Son:
inspire us, your children,
who are born of water and the Spirit,
to surrender our lives to your service,
that we may rejoice to be called the sons of God;
through Jesus Christ our Lord.

Christmas 4

Almighty God,
by whose grace alone we are accepted and called to your service:
strengthen us by your Holy Spirit
and make us worthy of our calling;
through Jesus Christ our Lord.

Christmas 5

Almighty God,
in Christ you make all things new.
Transform the poverty of our nature by the riches of your grace,
and in the renewal of our lives
make known your heavenly glory;
through Jesus Christ our Lord. (13b)

Christmas 6

Merciful Lord,
grant to your faithful people
pardon and peace:
that we may be cleansed from all our sins
and serve you with a quiet mind;
through Jesus Christ our Lord. (1)

Extra Sunday after Christmas

Give us, Lord, we pray,
the spirit to think and to do always those things that are right:
that we, who can do no good thing without you,
may have power to live according to your holy will;
through Jesus Christ our Lord. (1)

9 before Easter

Eternal God,
whose Son Jesus Christ is for all mankind
the way, the truth, and the life:
grant us to walk in his way,
to rejoice in his truth,
and to share his risen life;
who is alive and reigns with you and the Holy Spirit,
one God, now and for ever.

8 before Easter

Almighty and everliving God,
whose Son Jesus Christ healed the sick
and restored them to wholeness of life:
look with compassion on the anguish of the world,
and by your healing power
make whole both men and nations;
through our Lord and Saviour Jesus Christ,
who is alive and reigns with you and the Holy Spirit,
one God, now and for ever.

7 before Easter

Almighty God,
whose Son revealed in signs and miracles
the wonder of your saving love:
renew your people with your heavenly grace,
and in all our weakness
sustain us by your mighty power;
through Jesus Christ our Lord.

Ash Wednesday

Almighty and everlasting God,
you hate nothing that you have made
and forgive the sins of all those who are penitent.
Create and make in us new and contrite hearts,
that, lamenting our sins and acknowledging our wretchedness,
we may receive from you, the God of all mercy,
perfect forgiveness and peace;
through Jesus Christ our Lord. (1)

6 before Easter (Lent 1)

Almighty God,
whose Son Jesus Christ fasted forty days in the wilderness,
and was tempted as we are, yet without sin:
give us grace to discipline ourselves in obedience to your Spirit;
and, as you know our weakness,
so may we know your power to save;
through Jesus Christ our Lord.

5 before Easter (Lent 2)

Lord God Almighty,
grant your people grace
to withstand the temptations
  of the world, the flesh, and the devil,
and with pure hearts and minds
to follow you, the only God;
through Jesus Christ our Lord. (1)

4 before Easter (Lent 3)

Almighty God,
whose most dear Son went not up to joy
  but first he suffered pain,
and entered not into glory before he was crucified:
mercifully grant that we, walking in the way of the cross,
may find it none other than the way of life and peace;
through Jesus Christ our Lord. (16)

3 before Easter (Lent 4)

Almighty Father,
whose Son was revealed in majesty
  before he suffered death upon the cross:
give us faith to perceive his glory,
that we may be strengthened to suffer with him
and be changed into his likeness, from glory to glory;
who is alive and reigns with you and the Holy Spirit,
one God, now and for ever. (2)

2 before Easter (Passion Sunday)

Most merciful God,
who by the death and resurrection of your Son Jesus Christ
delivered and saved mankind:
grant that by faith in him who suffered on the cross,
we may triumph in the power of his victory;
through the same Jesus Christ our Lord.

Palm Sunday

Almighty and everlasting God,
who in your tender love towards mankind
sent your Son our Saviour Jesus Christ
to take upon him our flesh
and to suffer death upon the cross:
grant that we may follow the example
of his patience and humility,
and also be made partakers of his resurrection;
through Jesus Christ our Lord. (1)

Good Friday

Almighty Father,
look with mercy on this your family
for which our Lord Jesus Christ was content
to be betrayed
and given up into the hands of wicked men
and to suffer death upon the cross;
who is alive and glorified with you and the Holy Spirit,
one God, now and for ever. (1)

Easter Day

Lord of all life and power,
who through the mighty resurrection of your Son
overcame the old order of sin and death
to make all things new in him:
grant that we, being dead to sin
and alive to you in Jesus Christ,
may reign with him in glory;
to whom with you and the Holy Spirit
be praise and honour, glory and might,
now and in all eternity.

Easter 1

1 Almighty Father,
you gave your Son to die for us and to rise again,
that we may have life in him.
Grant that we may be nourished by his life
and strengthened to serve you in holiness and truth;
through Jesus Christ our Lord.

2 Almighty Father,
who in your great mercy made glad the disciples
with the sight of the risen Lord:
give us such knowledge of his presence with us,
that we may be strengthened and sustained by his risen life
and serve you continually in righteousness and truth;
through Jesus Christ our Lord.

Easter 2

1 Merciful Father,
you gave your Son Jesus Christ to be the good shepherd,
who in his love for us laid down his life and rose again:
keep us under his protection,
and give us grace to follow in his steps;
through the same Jesus Christ our Lord.

2 God of peace,
who brought again from the dead our Lord Jesus Christ,
that great shepherd of the sheep,
by the blood of the eternal covenant:
make us perfect in every good work to do your will,
and work in us that which is well-pleasing in your sight;
through Jesus Christ our Lord.

Easter 3

Almighty God,
whose Son Jesus Christ is the resurrection
and the life of all who put their trust in him:
raise us, we pray, from the death of sin
to the life of righteousness;
that we may seek the things which are above,
where he reigns with you and the Holy Spirit,
one God, now and for ever.

Easter 4

Almighty God,
who alone can bring order
to the unruly wills and passions of sinful men:
give us grace to love what you command
and to desire what you promise,
that in all the changes and chances of this world,
our hearts may surely there be fixed
where lasting joys are to be found;
through Jesus Christ our Lord. (1)

Easter 5

Almighty and everlasting God,
you are always more ready to hear than we to pray
and give more than either we desire or deserve.
Pour down upon us the abundance of your mercy,
forgiving us those things of which our conscience is afraid
and giving us those good things which we are not worthy to ask
save through the merits and mediation
of Jesus Christ your Son our Lord. (1)

Eternal Father,
whose Son Jesus Christ ascended to the throne of heaven
that he might rule over all things as Lord:
keep the Church in the unity of the Spirit
and in the bond of his peace,
and bring the whole created order to worship at his feet;
who is alive and reigns with you and the Holy Spirit,
one God, now and for ever.

Ascension Day

Almighty God,
as we believe your only-begotten Son our Lord Jesus Christ
to have ascended into the heavens,
so may we also in heart and mind thither ascend
and with him continually dwell;
who is alive and reigns with you and the Holy Spirit,
one God, now and for ever. (1)

Easter 6

Eternal God, the King of Glory,
you have exalted your only Son
with great triumph to your kingdom in heaven.
Leave us not comfortless,
but send your Holy Spirit to strengthen us
and exalt us to the place
where Christ is gone before,
and where with you and the Holy Spirit
he is worshipped and glorified,
now and for ever. (1)

Pentecost

1 Almighty God,
who at this time
taught the hearts of your faithful people
by sending to them the light of your Holy Spirit:
grant us by the same Spirit
to have a right judgement in all things,
and evermore to rejoice in his holy comfort;
through the merits of Christ Jesus our Saviour,
who is alive and reigns with you in the unity of the Spirit,
one God, now and for ever. (1)

2 Almighty God,
who on the day of Pentecost
sent your Holy Spirit to the disciples
with the wind from heaven and in tongues of flame,
filling them with joy and boldness to preach the gospel:
send us out in the power of the same Spirit
to witness to your truth
and to draw all men to the fire of your love;
through Jesus Christ our Lord.

Pentecost 1 (Trinity Sunday)

Almighty and eternal God,
you have revealed yourself as Father, Son, and Holy Spirit,
and live and reign in the perfect unity of love.
Hold us firm in this faith,
that we may know you in all your ways
and evermore rejoice in your eternal glory,
who are three Persons in one God,
now and for ever. (13a)

Pentecost 2

Almighty and everlasting God,
by whose Spirit the whole body of the Church
  is governed and sanctified:
hear our prayer which we offer for all your faithful people;
that each in his vocation and ministry
may serve you in holiness and truth
to the glory of your Name;
through our Lord and Saviour Jesus Christ. (1)

Pentecost 3

Lord God our Father,
through our Saviour Jesus Christ
you have assured mankind of eternal life
and in baptism have made us one with him.
Deliver us from the death of sin
and raise us to new life in your love,
in the fellowship of the Holy Spirit,
by the grace of our Lord Jesus Christ.

Pentecost 4

Almighty God,
you have broken the tyranny of sin
and have sent the Spirit of your Son into our hearts
whereby we call you Father.
Give us grace to dedicate our freedom to your service,
that all mankind may be brought
  to the glorious liberty of the sons of God;
through Jesus Christ our Lord.

Pentecost 5

Almighty God,
to those who are in error
you show the light of your truth,
that they may turn to the way of righteousness.
May we who have been admitted to the fellowship of Christ
reject what is false
and hold fast to the truth;
through Jesus Christ our Lord. (1)

Pentecost 6

1 Almighty God,
you have chosen us as your own
and you give us new life in Christ.
Fill us with his spirit of compassion and love,
and may his peace always reign in our hearts.
We ask this in his name and for his sake.

2 O God,
since without you
we are not able to please you:
mercifully grant that your Holy Spirit
may in all things direct and rule our hearts;
through Jesus Christ our Lord. (1)

Pentecost 7

Lord, you have taught us
that all our doings without love are nothing worth.
Send your Holy Spirit
and pour into our hearts that most excellent gift of love,
the true bond of peace and of all virtues,
without which whoever lives is counted dead before you.
Grant this for the sake of your only Son,
Jesus Christ our Lord. (1)

Pentecost 8

Almighty God,
who sent your Holy Spirit
to be the life and light of your Church:
open our hearts to the riches of his grace,
that we may bring forth the fruit of the Spirit
in love and joy and peace;
through Jesus Christ our Lord.

Pentecost 9

Almighty God,
you see that we have no power of ourselves to help ourselves.
Keep us both outwardly in our bodies
  and inwardly in our souls,
that we may be defended from all adversities
  which may happen to the body,
and from all evil thoughts
  which may assault and hurt the soul;
through Jesus Christ our Lord. (1)

Pentecost 10

Father of mankind,
who gave your only-begotten Son
to take upon himself the form of a servant
and to be obedient even to death on a cross:
give us the same mind that was in Christ Jesus
that, sharing his humility,
we may come to be with him in his glory;
who is alive and reigns with you and the Holy Spirit,
one God, now and for ever.

Pentecost 11

Almighty Father,
whose Son Jesus Christ has taught us
that what we do for the least of our brethren
we do also for him:
give us the will to be the servant of others
as he was the servant of all,
who gave up his life and died for us,
but is alive and reigns with you and the Holy Spirit,
one God, now and for ever.

Pentecost 12

Almighty God,
who called your Church to witness
that you were in Christ reconciling men to yourself:
help us so to proclaim the good news of your love,
that all who hear it may be reconciled to you;
through him who died for us and rose again
and reigns with you and the Holy Spirit,
one God, now and for ever.

Pentecost 13

1 God our Father,
you have called us into your service.
Grant that, if we must suffer for Christ's sake,
we may be faithful in all adversity
and endure with courage to the end;
through Christ our Lord.

2 Lord God,
whose blessed Son our Saviour
gave his back to the smiters
and did not hide his face from shame:
give us grace to endure the sufferings of this present time
with sure confidence in the glory that shall be revealed;
through Jesus Christ our Lord. (16a)

Pentecost 14

Almighty God,
you have taught us through your Son
that love is the fulfilling of the law.
Grant that we may love you with our whole heart
and our neighbours as ourselves;
through Jesus Christ our Lord.

Pentecost 15

Lord God,
the protector of all who trust in you,
without whom nothing is strong, nothing is holy:
increase and multiply upon us your mercy,
that you being our ruler and guide,
we may so pass through things temporal
that we finally lose not the things eternal.
Grant this, heavenly Father,
for the sake of Jesus Christ our Lord. (1)

Pentecost 16

Almighty Father,
whose will is to restore all things
in your beloved Son, the king of all:
govern the hearts and minds of those in authority,
and bring the families of the nations,
divided and torn apart by the ravages of sin,
to be subject to his just and gentle rule;
who is alive and reigns with you and the Holy Spirit,
one God, now and for ever.

Pentecost 17

Lord of all power and might,
the author and giver of all good things:
graft in our hearts the love of your Name,
increase in us true religion,
nourish in us all goodness,
and of your great mercy keep us in the same;
through Jesus Christ our Lord. (1)

Pentecost 18

Almighty God,
you have made us for yourself,
and our hearts are restless
till they find their rest in you.
Teach us to offer ourselves to your service,
that here we may have your peace,
and in the world to come may see you face to face;
through Jesus Christ our Lord.

Pentecost 19

Merciful God,
you have prepared for those who love you
such good things as pass man's understanding.
Pour into our hearts such love towards you
that we, loving you above all things,
may obtain your promises,
which exceed all that we can desire;
through Jesus Christ our Lord. (1)

Pentecost 20

Almighty God,
your Son has opened for us
a new and living way into your presence.
Give us pure hearts and steadfast wills
to worship you in spirit and in truth;
through the same Jesus Christ our Lord.

Pentecost 21

Lord God,
the protector of all who trust in you,
without whom nothing is strong, nothing is holy:
increase and multiply upon us your mercy,
that you being our ruler and guide,
we may so pass through things temporal
that we finally lose not the things eternal.
Grant this, heavenly Father,
for the sake of Jesus Christ our Lord. (1)

Extra Sundays after Pentecost

1 Lord God,
we ask you to keep your household the Church
always true to its calling:
that through your grace and protection,
it may be set free from all adversities
and serve you in all that is good;
through Jesus Christ our Lord. (1)

2 Stir up, O Lord,
the wills of your faithful people;
that richly bearing the fruit of good works,
they may by you be richly rewarded;
through Jesus Christ our Lord. (1)

A WEEKLY CYCLE OF INTERCESSIONS AND THANKSGIVINGS

MONDAY

Creation in Christ: Creation and Providence

1 Almighty God,
Maker of all things and Father of us all,
you have shown us in Christ the purpose of your creation
and called us to responsible service in the world.

2 INTERCESSION

We pray for THE WORLD

all nations . . .
our own country . . .
the peace of the world . . .
racial harmony and justice . . .
reverence for the earth . . .

3 THANKSGIVING

We give thanks

for the order and beauty of created things
the resources of the earth
the gift of human life . . .
for the continuing work of creation
our share in it
creative vision and inventive skill . . .
for your faithfulness to us in patience and in love
every human response of obedience
and humble achievement . . .

4 May we share your delight
in all that you have made,
discern your providence
even in our pain,
and work to bring all things
to their true end;
through Jesus Christ our Lord. **Amen.**

TUESDAY

The Incarnate Life of Christ: Revelation and Human Knowledge

1 God our Father,
you gave your Son, Jesus Christ
to share our life on earth,
to grow in wisdom,
to toil with his hands, and
to make known the ways of your kingdom.

2 INTERCESSION

We pray for SOCIETY

those who work . . .
the unemployed . . .
those in education . . .
those in research . . .
those in communication . . .
those who maintain the life of the community . . .

3 THANKSGIVING

We give thanks

for his revelation of yourself
his care for people
his joy in obedience . . .
for the value he gave to human labour
the strength he promised us for service
the call to follow in his way . . .
for all opportunities of work and of leisure
all truth that we have learned
all discoveries that man has made . . .

4 Give us growing reverence for the truth,
and such wisdom in the use of knowledge,
that your kingdom may be advanced,
and your name glorified;
through Jesus Christ our Lord. **Amen.**

WEDNESDAY

The Cross of Christ: Reconciliation and Human Relationships

1 Holy Father,
you have reconciled us to yourself in Christ,
who is the same, yesterday, today, and for ever,
and eternally pleads our cause.

2 INTERCESSION

We pray for PERSONAL RELATIONSHIPS

the home and family life . . .
children deprived of home . . .
friends and relations . . .
neighbours . . .
relationships in daily life and work . . .
those who are estranged.

3 THANKSGIVING

We give thanks

for the intercession of Christ to which our prayers are joined
his care for his people
his mercy for the world, which never fails . . .
for the joy of human love and friendship
the lives to which our own are bound
the gift of peace with you and each other . . .
for the communities in whose life we share
all relationships in which reconciliation may be known . . .

4 Help us to share in Christ's ministry
and to be the agents of his compassion,
that we may love and serve one another in peace;
through the same Jesus Christ our Lord,
who in the unity of the Spirit is one with you for ever. **Amen.**

THURSDAY

The Resurrection of Christ:
The Divine Society, the Church

1 Eternal God,
you have raised Jesus Christ from the dead
and exalted him to your right hand in glory,
and through him called your Church into being,
that your people might know you, and
that they might make your name known.

2 INTERCESSION

We pray for THE CHURCH

the Church, universal and local . . .
the unity of the Church . . .
the ministries of the Church . . .
the mission of the Church . . .
the renewal of the Church . . .
all Christians in this place . . .

3 THANKSGIVING

We give thanks

for the apostolic gospel committed to your Church
the continuing presence and power of your Spirit
the ministry of word, sacrament, and prayer . . .
for the divine mission in which we are called to share
the will to unity and its fruit in common action
the faithful witness of those who are true to Christ . . .
for all works of Christian compassion
every service that proclaims your love . . .

4 In peace and unity
may your people offer the unfailing sacrifice of praise,
and make your glory known;
through Jesus Christ our Lord. **Amen.**

FRIDAY

The Priestly Ministry of Christ:
All that meets Human Need

1 Gracious God and Father,
you have given your Son for us all,
that his death might be our life
and his affliction our peace.

2 INTERCESSION

We pray for THE SUFFERING

the hungry . . .
the refugees . . .
the prisoners . . .
the persecuted . . .
agents of sin and suffering . . .
ministries of care and relief . . .

3 THANKSGIVING

We give thanks

for the cross of Christ at the heart of creation
the presence of Christ in our weakness and strength
the power of Christ to transform our suffering . . .
for all ministries of healing
all agencies of relief
all that sets men free from pain, fear, and distress . . .
for the assurance that your mercy knows no limit
the privilege of sharing your work of renewal
through prayer . . .

4 In darkness and in light,
in trouble and in joy,
help us to trust your love,
to serve your purpose, and
to praise your name;
through Jesus Christ our Lord. **Amen.**

SATURDAY

Consummation in Christ:
The Fulfilment of the Divine Purpose

1 Eternal God,
you have declared in Christ
the completion of all your purpose of love.

2 INTERCESSION

We pray for THE SICK AND THE DEPARTED
the tempted and despairing . . .
the sick and handicapped . . .
the aged . . .
the ministries of care and healing . . .
those who mourn . . .
the departed . . .

3 THANKSGIVING

We give thanks
for the triumphs of the gospel that herald your salvation
the signs of renewal that declare
the coming of your kingdom
the human lives that reveal your work of grace . . .
for the unceasing praise of the company of heaven
the promise to those who mourn that
all tears shall be wiped away,
the pledge of death destroyed and victory won . . .
for our foretaste of eternal life through baptism and eucharist
our hope in the Spirit
the communion of saints . . .

4 May we live by faith, walk in hope, and be renewed in love,
until the world reflects your glory
and you are all in all.
Even so, come Lord Jesus. **Amen.**

A CYCLE OF INTERCESSIONS FOR THE MISSION OF THE CHURCH

These intercessions
may be used seasonally
or on a weekly basis

A CYCLE OF INTERCESSIONS FOR THE MISSION OF THE CHURCH

1

Almighty Father, you give us life
as you give life to all people.
You call us into the Church
that with men and women
of different race, colour, and language,
different experience and different traditions,
we may be one body
to the glory of Christ on earth.
Help us to be what you have called us to be.

Minister You are the giver of life.
***People* Father, renew us by your Spirit.**

Father of all men, you give us
wealth in the earth and in the oceans,
forests and fertile plains,
air to breathe, water to drink,
and all that is needful for human life.
We pray for those who know little of your bounty,
for whom the earth is a cruel desert
and existence a constant struggle
against overwhelming odds.
We acknowledge that their burdens should be our burdens;
we acknowledge that we share a common humanity.

Minister You are the giver of life.
***People* Father, renew us by your Spirit.**

Father, you have so made us that we need one another,
but because we do not know how to love all men
you tell us to start with the sister or brother at our side.
We pray for any from whom we are estranged. Bless them;
and bless us in our future relationships with them.
We pray for our families, our friends,
and all whom we meet day by day . . .

In their particular needs we ask you to bless them.
Minister You are the giver of life.
People **Father, renew us by your Spirit.**

Father, you are present in every part of human experience.
We hold before you
the infant lying in his mother's arms,
the young lovers planning together their first home,
the sick and infirm battling with weakness and incapacity,
the dying, soon to experience your new creation.
Minister You are the giver of life.
People **Father, renew us by your Spirit.**

Eternal Father, we remember before you
those who have passed from this world . . .
As we all received from you the gift of life
so we pray that you will bring us to the life eternal.
Minister You are the giver of life.
People **Father, renew us by your Spirit.**

2

We pray for the Church,
where all too often we, like Cain,
have made the worship offered by our brother
a cause for hostility and division.
We pray that our Lord may bind us together,
teaching us to value the richness of our diversity
and to rejoice in every fresh glimpse of God's glory
seen through traditions other than our own.
Minister Lord, teach us to love:
People **That we may be children of God.**

We pray for those lands where brother fights brother,
divided by arbitrary borders, ideology or religion.
We pray for those lands where extremes of wealth and poverty
are bitterly divisive.

We pray for those lands where power is grossly abused
and the dispossessed bear the heaviest burden.

Minister Lord, teach us to love:
People **That we may be children of God.**

We pray for all who have been nourished on bitterness
and fed with the wrongs suffered by earlier generations.
We pray for all who have grown to hate people
instead of hating that which evil has done to people.
We pray for the young who are impatient for change
and the not so young who resist all change.

Minister Lord, teach us to love:
People **That we may be children of God.**

We commend to God any special needs known to us . . .
As we remember the sick, the sorrowful, and all who are
in any distress,
let us also remember that God has supremely made himself
known to us as Saviour
and calls us to share in his rescuing work.

Minister Lord, teach us to love:
People **That we may be children of God.**

Lord, we would heal and not destroy.
Teach us the discipline of obedience to the commandment
'You shall love your neighbour as yourself',
and give us the fortitude to go on obeying to the end.

Minister Lord, teach us to love:
People **That we may be children of God.**

Let us remember before God those who have died . . .
Lord we are all sinners and utterly dependent on your grace.
We praise you for the forgiveness of sins
by which men and women are enabled
to rise from death to eternal life.

Minister Lord, teach us to love:
People **That we may be children of God.**

3

Lord, we often fold our hands in prayer,
when we should really jump for joy
because you come to us as rescuer, as Saviour,
cleaning up the mess we make of our lives,
putting together what we pull apart.

Minister Tell out, my soul, the greatness of the Lord.
***People* Rejoice, my spirit, in God my Saviour.**

We pray for the Church.
You have called us to have a part in its life
and despite our failures, you have not cast us off.

Minister Tell out, my soul, the greatness of the Lord.
***People* Rejoice, my spirit, in God my Saviour.**

We know that much of the Church's life and witness
looks silly and weak in the eyes of the world at large,
but you still use its foolishness to shame worldly wisdom
and its weakness to witness against the abuse of power.

Minister Tell out, my soul, the greatness of the Lord.
***People* Rejoice, my spirit, in God my Saviour.**

We pray for those who cry desperately for salvation
    for tyranny to be overthrown
    for the despised to be given dignity
    for the poor to receive a proper share
        of the earth's resources.
You are the source of hope and the inspiration to action.

Minister Tell out, my soul, the greatness of the Lord.
***People* Rejoice, my spirit, in God my Saviour.**

We bring you particular needs . . .
With confidence we share these with you
for you are the God who lives amongst us.

Minister Tell out, my soul, the greatness of the Lord.
***People* Rejoice, my spirit, in God my Saviour.**

We pray for our families . . .
Your human life brought both pain and joy
to your earthly relatives.
Help us also to know you in both the joys and the pains
of family life.

Minister Tell out, my soul, the greatness of the Lord.
People **Rejoice, my spirit, in God my Saviour.**

We remember those who have died . . .
Through our sorrow and sense of loss we are glad
for the promise that there shall be an end to death,
and to mourning and crying and pain;
that the old order has passed away.

Minister Tell out, my soul, the greatness of the Lord.
People **Rejoice, my spirit, in God my Saviour.**

4

Lord Jesus, you have faced temptation,
you know how difficult it can be
to distinguish between vision and mirage,
between truth and falsehood.

Minister Lord, help us when we are tempted:
People **And save us when we fall.**

Help us in the Church—
When we confuse absence of conflict with the peace of God.
When we equate the shaping of ecclesiastical structures with
serving you in the world.
When we imagine that our task is to preserve
rather than to put at risk.
When we behave as though your presence in life were a past
event rather than a contemporary encounter.

Minister Lord, help us when we are tempted:
People **And save us when we fall.**

Help us in the world—
When we use meaningless chatter to avoid real dialogue.

When we allow the image presented by the media to blind us to the substance that lies behind it.
When we confuse privilege with responsibility and claim rights when we should be acknowledging duties.
When we allow high sounding reasons to cover evil actions.

Minister Lord, help us when we are tempted:
People **And save us when we fall.**

We pray for our families and our friends and hold them before you in our thoughts . . .
We especially pray for any who may be under particular pressures at this time . . .

Minister Lord, help us when we are tempted:
People **And save us when we fall.**

Lord Jesus, you have passed through the test of suffering
and are able to help those who are meeting their test now.
We pray for all who suffer . . .
We especially pray for those who suffer through their own folly or the folly or malice of other men.

Minister Lord, help us when we are tempted:
People **And save us when we fall.**

Before the throne of God, where we may find mercy and timely help,
we remember those who have departed this life . . .
Dying, Christ broke the power of sin and death
that we might enter with him into the life eternal.

Minister Lord, help us when we are tempted:
People **And save us when we fall.**

5

Crucified and risen Lord,
we pray for the Church.
Save us from dawdling by an empty tomb.
Save us from bondage to the past.
Save us from the hypnotic fascination of decay and death
and make your Church to know your resurrection life.
May we follow where you lead
and live for you in today's world.

Minister The Lord is risen.
***People* He is risen indeed.**

Saviour Christ, we pray for mankind.
Hanging on the cross
you gave hope to a rebel at your side
and prayed for those who condemned you to that violent death.
We too live amid violence,
the violence of subversion, of repressive government,
and all the subtle violence by which the powerful
seek to impose their will on the weak.
None of us is free from its taint.
You alone can give victory over the violence of the world
and of our hearts.
Save us, Lord.
Give us the will and the power to share your victory.

Minister The Lord is risen.
***People* He is risen indeed.**

Living Lord, we pray for our society,
entombed in material possessions
and oppressed with ever-changing fears.
Many know no better hope than that things may get no worse
and that they may enjoy a few years of quiet retirement
before the end.
Release us from this living death!
Cause us to live with the life you alone can give!

Minister The Lord is risen.
***People* He is risen indeed.**

Lord, you know what it is to suffer pain, degradation,
and rejection and to die an outcast.
We pray for all who suffer . . .
May they know you as one who shares their agony
and enables them to share your triumph.

Minister The Lord is risen.
***People* He is risen indeed.**

With thanksgiving for the life that was given
and joyous hope of the life that is yet to be
we remember those who have died . . .
As in Adam all men die,
so in Christ will all be brought to life.

Minister The Lord is risen.
***People* He is risen indeed.**

6

Spirit of power,
we find it hard to come together in the Church
even within a single congregation.
How shall we learn to be one family
loving and serving the whole of mankind?
Lead us into such unity of purpose
that we may receive power:
not the power to threaten or destroy
but the power to restore waste places.
Use us to declare your glory
that blind eyes may see, deaf ears hear,
and the cynical be brought to faith.

Minister Spirit of the Living God,
***People* Hear our prayer.**

Spirit of truth,
we live in a modern Babel
where words are used to conceal meaning
rather than make it plain.
Lead the peoples of the world into such a love of truth
that nation may speak with nation,
not seeking to confuse
but to understand and to be understood,
whereby trust is created, out of which
a truly international community may be born.

Minister Spirit of the Living God,
***People* Hear our prayer.**

Creator Spirit,
you give men the capacity
to dream dreams and to see visions,
but because we exalt ourselves and our desires
to the place that is yours alone,
our visions are visions of horror
and our dreams nightmares.
Raise up artists and prophets among us
with the will and the ability
to inspire and cleanse our society,
to set our hearts aflame and turn our eyes to the heights.

Minister Spirit of the Living God,
***People* Hear our prayer.**

Source of all comfort, we pray for the lonely, the sick, the sad,
the bereaved and all who suffer or are ill at ease . . .
We claim for them the gift of your peace,
that their troubled hearts may be set at rest
and their fears banished.

Minister Spirit of the Living God,
***People* Hear our prayer.**

Giver of life, we remember those who have died . . .
May they enter into the Kingdom
where your presence is all in all.

Minister Spirit of the Living God,
***People* Hear our prayer.**

7

Lord Jesus, in a dark hour
you spoke of the gift of peace;
we beg that gift for ourselves, that we may have
the inner serenity that cannot be taken from us,
then we may be messengers of your peace
to a strife-torn world.

Minister Give peace in our time, Lord.
***People* Help us to live in peace.**

We pray for those who are fighting,
injury, disfigurement, and death their constant companions,
nerves and bodies strained beyond endurance,
the streams of compassion drying up within them,
their only goal the destruction of the 'enemy'.
Whatever the colour of their skin—we pray for them.
Whatever the sound of their tongue—we pray for them.
Whatever the insignia they wear—we pray for them.

Minister Give peace in our time, Lord.
***People* Help us to live in peace.**

We pray for all who have been broken in battle;
for those who weep and those who can no longer weep;
for those who feel the anguish and for those who have lost the capacity to feel;
for all prisoners—and all gaolers;
for those who exist in war-torn lands and for those who no longer have a homeland.

Minister Give peace in our time, Lord.
***People* Help us to live in peace.**

We pray for all who stir up strife;
for all who make a profit out of the misery of others;
for all who are led into vice
as they seek a momentary forgetfulness;
for all who believe that war is inevitable.

Minister Give peace in our time, Lord.
People **Help us to live in peace.**

The desire to press self-interest is deeply rooted in us.
We defend our attitudes when we should be ashamed of them.
We compare the noblest aspects of our own cause with the basest of that of our opponents.
We are reluctant to admit that our own selfish desires could contribute to the miseries of others.

Minister Give peace in our time, Lord.
People **Help us to live in peace.**

We bring to you particular needs . . .
and we remember those who have died . . .

O Lord, support us all the day long of this troubled life, until the shades lengthen, and the evening comes, and the busy world is hushed, the fever of life over, and our work done. Then, Lord, in thy mercy grant us safe lodging, a holy rest, and peace at the last; through Jesus Christ our Lord. **Amen.** (2)

Minister Give peace in our time, Lord.
People **Help us to live in peace.**

PRAYERS ON VARIOUS OCCASIONS

A PRAYER OF ADORATION

O God all-powerful, true and incomparable,
present in all things, yet limited by none,
untouched by place,
unaged by time,
unhurried by the years,
undeceived by words,
not subject to birth
nor in need of protection:
you are above all corruption,
you are beyond all change,
you are by nature immutable,
living in light that none can approach,
invisible, yet you make yourself known to me
and you are found by all who seek you with their whole heart;
you are the God of Israel
and of all who hope in Christ. (31)

Come to us in your Holy Sacrament Through Jesus Christ Our Lord

Minister You are our God.
People **We adore you.**

PENITENCE

A GENERAL ACT OF PENITENCE

We acknowledge before God the Lord
  the wretchedness of our world
  and the sins of our hearts and minds.
Our times are full of evil
  and we are but children of our times.
We have seen the light and we are party to darkness.
We have seen the truth and are but half-believers.
We are disciples, but poor disciples
  unable to give sight to our neighbour
  who is blind to where blessing lies.
We confess these things with shame
  and pray God to forgive and redeem.

God, have mercy upon us.

(Silence)

Almighty God, have mercy upon us,
pardon and deliver us from all our sins,
confirm and strengthen us in all goodness,
and keep us in life eternal;
through Jesus Christ our Lord. Amen.

A MUTUAL CONFESSION

Have mercy on us, O God, in your goodness;
in your great tenderness wipe away our faults.
Wash us clean of our guilt;
purify us from our sin.
God, create a clean heart in us;
put into us a new and constant spirit.
Be our saviour again, renew our joy,
keep our spirit steady and willing.

THE DECLARATION OF FORGIVENESS

The almighty and merciful God grant us pardon and remission of all our sins, time for amendment of life, and the grace and comfort of the Holy Spirit. Amen.

A GENERAL THANKSGIVING

Almighty God, we give you thanks
  for this life and all its blessings,
  for joys great and simple,
  for gifts and powers more than we deserve,
  for love at the heart of your purpose
  and a surpassing wisdom in all your works,
  for light in the world
  brought once in Christ and shining ever through his Spirit.
We pray, through Jesus Christ our Lord,
  for that light to dawn upon us daily,
  that we may always have a grateful heart,
  and a will to love and to serve
  to the end of our days.
Lord, hear our prayer and our praises:
Alleluia, we bless you, O God.

ACCLAMATIONS AND AFFIRMATIONS

1 Christ has died.
Christ is risen.
In Christ shall all be made alive.

Blessing and honour and glory and power be to our God for ever and ever.

2 Christ is Victor.
Christ is King.
Christ is Lord of all.

3 Praise the Lord!
Dying you destroyed our death.
Rising you restored our life.
Lord Jesus, come in glory.

4 Blessed be God the Father, Creator of all.
Blessed be God the Son, Christ confessed of men.
Blessed be God the Holy Spirit, Lord and giver of life.

5 The Son of Man suffers and is rejected.
You are the Christ; you can make us free.
The Son of Man will come in his Father's glory.
You are his Son, the Beloved. We will listen to you.
The Son of Man has been killed and is risen from the dead.
Lord, we have faith; help us where faith falls short.

6 Christ humbled himself,
and became obedient unto death,
even death on a cross.
Therefore God has highly exalted him,
and bestowed on him the name
which is above every name.

7 Blessed art thou, O God the Father,
Creator of all things.
Blessed art thou, O Lord Jesus Christ, Son of God,
baptized in Jordan, crucified at Calvary, risen and glorified.
Blessed art thou, O Holy Spirit of God,
Lord and giver of life. (17)

8 God is Spirit, and those who worship him
must worship him in spirit and in truth.
God is Light, and if we walk in the light, we have fellowship.
God is Love, and he who loves is born of God and knows God.

9 Praise be to the God and Father of our Lord Jesus Christ.
In his mercy he gives us new birth into a living hope by the resurrection of Jesus Christ from the dead.

10 All who are moved by the Spirit are sons of God.
The Spirit aids our weakness,
pleading for God's own people in God's own way.
Our sufferings are as nothing to the freedom of God's children.
Nothing can separate us from God's love,
in Jesus Christ our Lord.
The victory is ours.
The Spirit sets us free.

11 Thou art worthy, O Lord our God, to receive glory and honour and power, because thou didst create all things; by thy will they were created, and have their being!
Amen! Praise and glory and wisdom, thanksgiving and honour, power and might, be to our God for ever and ever! Amen!

The foregoing forms of acclamation and affirmation are intentionally brief. As such they have a number of possible uses in worship. The following might be examples:

(*a*) At the beginning of worship, as sentences calling to worship, or as introductions to prayer of adoration, possibly silent prayer (Affirmation is the foothills of the Mount of Adoration).
(*b*) As a 'theme item' short enough to be repeated at several points in a

service, or several times during a prayer as a corporate response (e.g., a Thanksgiving Prayer). For this purpose they could usefully be set to music.

(*c*) As an alternative 'theme item' to a collect, say as an ascription after a sermon.

(*d*) As a post-communion acclamation or a pre-dismissal sentence.

(*e*) At a Baptism, (8) might be used after the baptismal blessing; at a Confirmation, (4) might be used after the confirmation prayer.

LITANIES

A LITANY OF INTERCESSION

Let us pray to God for one another and for all men,
that God will be merciful to us.

God the Father have mercy on us.
God the Son have mercy on us.
God the Holy Spirit have mercy on us.

Support us, O Lord, when we stumble;
Raise us up when we are weighed down.
Give to us the peace that comes from above,
And lead us in the path of truth.

Let us pray for the renewing of men's minds, so that they can discern the will of God;
Let us pray for heads of state and for the Queen;
Let us pray for men and women who influence the life of the nation (*or* region *or* district):

Lord, in your mercy
Hear our prayer.

Let us pray for those who face hazards and for all who suffer;
Let us pray for a holy and happy death, and rest in paradise for all the saints of God:

Lord, in your mercy
Hear our prayer.

Let us pray for the varied ministries of the Church today;
Let us pray God to give grace to the Church, to bind her to her Lord that she may serve him better and love men more;
Let us pray God to send the Spirit upon the Church that in all her words and works she may banish darkness and bring to birth new life upon the earth:

Lord, in your mercy
Hear our prayer.

A LITANY OF THANKSGIVING

Give thanks to God, for he is good. His love is everlasting!

For the gift of Christ the Lord:
Thanks be to God.

For the truth of the gospel that routs the cynicism and pessimism that assail us:
Thanks be to God.

For the power through grace to discern the goodness of the world and rejoice in it:
Thanks be to God.

For joy in beauty, in splendid sights, in glorious sounds:
Thanks be to God.

For joy in truth and love and all things of abiding quality:
Thanks be to God.

For the call of God to replenish the earth, and the challenge to share constructively in his creative work:
Thanks be to God.

For the mystery of the sacraments and the privilege of prayer:
Thanks be to God.

For the right to become the sons of God
through Christ our brother:
Thanks be to God.

For the heritage of faith enhanced by the passing of time
and by every new experience of the Holy Spirit:
Thanks be to God.

For the call to share with Christ in his continuing ministry of love,
and the challenge to work with him in redeeming the times:
Thanks be to God.

For the friendship of Christ and the companionship
of all his saints:
Thanks be to God.

For the blessings of every day and the hope of glory:
Thanks be to God.

Give thanks to God, for he is good: his love is everlasting!

A LITANY OF SUPPLICATION

If the Son sets you free, you will indeed be free.
Enable us, O God, gratefully to believe what the Scriptures openly declare.
The Jerusalem above, which is the mother of us all, is free.
Teach us, O God, to love that Jerusalem as the greatest of our joys.

From the evils of this world and the subtleties of sin:
Lord, set us free.
From what is artificial, shoddy, and insincere:
Lord, set us free.
From what is lazy, cowardly, and slack:
Lord, set us free.
From what is compromised and second-rate:
Lord, set us free.
From what is dishonourable and mean:
Lord, set us free.
From hatred and prejudice:
Lord, set us free.
From arrogance and pride:
Lord, set us free.
From self-indulgence and self-pity:
Lord, set us free.
From casualness about the things of God:
Lord, set us free.
From all our secret sins:
Lord, set us free.

Bind us to your service, O God, and we shall be free.
Give us by grace the rewards of your kingdom
and keep us in life eternal;
through Jesus Christ our Lord. **Amen.**

LITANY FOR CHRISTIAN UNITY

1

Let us ask the Holy Spirit
to kindle in us the fire of his love,
that his gifts may live and grow in his Church,
and everything may perish that opposes his will.

Lord, hear our prayer.

Let us ask the Holy Spirit
to inspire all who work and pray
for the unity of Christians,
and to guide them into all the truth.

Lord, hear our prayer.

Let us ask the Holy Spirit
to open our hearts
that Jesus may pray in us
his prayer for the unity of his brethren,
and lift us up together
in union with him.

Lord, hear our prayer.

Let us ask the Holy Spirit
to give us a share in the sufferings of our Lord,
caused by our disunion and infidelity,
that we may share also
in the power of his resurrection.

Lord, hear our prayer.

Let us ask the Holy Spirit
that the Church on earth may be ready, like the Lord,
to give her life for men,
and to be crushed by the weight of their needs,
that the kingdom of our God may come.

Lord, hear our prayer. Amen. (18)

LITANY FOR CHRISTIAN UNITY

2

With one voice and one heart let us pray to God our Father, who has gathered together his scattered children by the death and resurrection of his Son.

For the holy Church of God,
that Christians in their diversity
may learn to respect one another,
to understand one another,
and to love one another
as members of the body of Christ,
let us pray to the Lord.

Lord, hear us.

For the shepherds of all Christian flocks,
that God our Lord may help them
and those committed to their care
to be united in one faith and one love,
so that all the peoples of the world may believe,
let us pray to the Lord.

Lord, hear us.

For the Christians of all communions
persecuted for their faith,
that they may unite their suffering
to the sacrifice of Christ on the cross
and obtain the gift of unity,
let us pray to the Lord.

Lord, hear us.

For all the work undertaken in common
by separated Christians,
that it may lead to full communion,
let us pray to the Lord.

Lord, hear us.

Into your hands, our Father, we commit this your world, this your family, for which our Lord Jesus Christ was contented to be betrayed, and to suffer death upon the cross. Into your hands we commit your universal Church and her unity. Into your hands we commit all the problems which seem insoluble, in sure and certain hope, for in you is our trust. Here and now we lay all in your hands. All love, all glory, be unto you, for ever and ever. **Amen.**

We are all the more brothers and sisters, the more we live as children of God; therefore let us say with one voice:
Our Father . . .

The Lord be with you.
And also with you.

May the one God, Father Son, and Holy Spirit, draw us together and preserve us in unity now and for ever. **Amen.**

PRAYERS AT BAPTISM

Almighty God,
as you once delivered your chosen people
from slavery in Egypt,
and by your mercy brought them within the Old Covenant,
deliver those who are baptized into your Church
from all slavery to sin;
that through the New Covenant of your grace
they may receive the promise of eternal life
which you have given us in your Son
Jesus Christ our Lord. **Amen.** (13b)

Grant, O Lord,
that all those who are buried by baptism
into the death of your Son
may partake of his joyful resurrection;
and that, dying daily to sin
and rising again to the fullness of life,
they may serve you faithfully
in the fellowship of your saints
until, by your grace,
they inherit with them
the glory of your heavenly kingdom;
through Christ our Lord. **Amen.** (19)

God of all grace,
your Son was baptized
in the waters of the Jordan
and anointed with the Spirit.
May all who are buried with Christ
in the death of baptism
rise also with him to newness of life.
We ask this through Christ our Lord. **Amen.** (20)

Father, look now with love upon your Church,
and unseal for her the fountain of baptism;
that by the power of the Holy Spirit
your children may receive
the grace of your only Son
and come to a new birth
in your likeness;
through Jesus Christ our Lord. **Amen.** (20)

Eternal God,
we ask you to work within those
who have been born of water and the Spirit;
that, as through baptism
they have been incorporated
into Christ's new creation,
so by the power of the same Holy Spirit
they may share in his royal priesthood
and continue as his faithful witnesses;
through the same Christ our Lord. **Amen.**

O God,
as you have safely brought your children
into the ark of Christ's Church
through the waters of baptism,
grant them by your grace
so to wear the white robe of nnocence;
that they may come at last
to the glory of your kingdom;
through Christ our Lord. **Amen.**

Eternal Lord God,
who once entrusted to faithful parents
the well-being of your beloved Son;
grant your blessing to the homes of the newly baptized,
that by your grace
your children may come to know the joy
and to share the glory
of your perfect love;
through Jesus Christ our Lord. **Amen.**

Almighty God,
whose dear Son promised the Holy Spirit
to all who followed him;
pour out your gifts of grace
on those whom you have declared to be your children,
that, being born of water and the Spirit,
they may become in him
a new creation;
through Christ our Lord. **Amen.**

God our Father,
in your Son you have commanded us to baptize all nations.
Accept those whom we baptize in this sacrament,
and grant that they may be united to Christ in his Church
and receive, according to his promise,
the forgiveness of sins
and the gift of the Holy Spirit;
through the same Christ our Lord. **Amen.** (22)

PRAYERS FOR USE AT WEDDINGS

GENERAL

Minister Grace comes from you, O God, and you alone are the source of eternal life. Bless your servants *N* and *N*, that they may live together faithfully to the end of their lives.

Be with them in all their happiness, that your joy may be in them, and their joy may be full.

Strengthen them in times of trouble, that they may bear each other's burdens and so fulfil your law of love. **Amen.**

Minister Let your blessing be on their home:

People **That your peace may dwell there.**

Minister Let it be a place of welcome:

People **That its happiness may be freely shared.**

Minister Bless the families and friends of *N* and *N*:

People **That we may be united in love and friendship.**

Minister Now to him who is able to keep you from falling and to present you faultless before the presence of his glory with rejoicing;

People **To the only God, our saviour, through Jesus Christ our Lord, be glory, majesty, dominion and power, both now and for ever. Amen.** (23)

O Lord, our heavenly Father, who art the giver of all good gifts, build thou the home of these thy servants. Make them loving and patient, forgiving as each stands in need of forgiveness; make them rich in mutual understanding and forbearance, in courtesy and kindness; and grant that in their home thy law of love may reign, bringing to them a foretaste of thy Kingdom; through Jesus Christ our Lord. **Amen.**

FOR GOD'S BLESSING ON A MARRIAGE

Almighty God, look graciously, we pray, on this man and this woman, and on all whom you make to be one flesh in holy marriage. Make their lives together a sacrament of love to this broken world, so that unity may overcome estrangement, forgiveness heal guilt, and joy triumph over despair; in the name of our Lord Jesus Christ, to whom be all honour and glory, now and for ever. **Amen.**

Almighty God, giver of life and love, bless *N* and *N*, whom you have now joined in holy matrimony. Grant them wisdom and devotion in the ordering of their common life, that each may be to the other a strength in need, a counsellor in perplexity, a comfort in sorrow, and a companion in joy. And so knit their wills together in your will, and their spirits in your spirit, that they may live together in love and peace all the days of their life; through Jesus Christ our Lord. **Amen.**

Almighty God, by whose love the whole world is created, sustained, and redeemed, so fill *N* and *N* with the overflowing abundance of your grace that their lives may reflect your compassion for all men. May their love for each other not blind them to the brokenness in the world. As you teach them to bind up each other's wounds, teach them also to heal the hurts of others. As their mutual respect orders their common life within the family, direct them to their share also in the shaping of a society in which human dignity may flourish and abound. At all times and in all seasons may they rejoice to serve you and to give you thanks, through Jesus Christ our Lord. **Amen.** (24)

Minister Blessed are you, heavenly Father:
People **You give joy to bridegroom and bride.**
Minister Blessed are you, Lord Jesus Christ:
People **You have brought new life to mankind.**
Minister Blessed are you, Holy Spirit of God:
People **You bring us together in love.**
Minister Blessed be Father, Son, and Holy Spirit:
People **One God, to be praised for ever. Amen.** (25)

AFTER THE VOWS

God our Father,
you have enabled *N* and *N*
to make these great and solemn vows.
Help them to know
that it is not their beginning of marriage,
but its continuance until they are made fully perfect
that brings true glory;
through Jesus Christ our Lord. **Amen.**

Almighty God, in whom we live and move and have our being; look graciously upon the world which you have made, and on the Church for which your Son gave his life; and especially on all whom you make to be one flesh in holy marriage. Grant that their lives together may be a sacrament of your love to this broken world, so that unity may overcome estrangement, forgiveness heal guilt, and joy overcome despair; through Jesus Christ our Lord. **Amen.**

Grant that *N* and *N* may so live together, that the strength of their love may enrich our common life and become an example of your faithfulness. **Amen.**

Grant that they may have children, if it be your will, and may bring them up by your help to know and love you. **Amen.**

Grant them such fulfilment of their mutual affection that they may reach out in concern for others, to the praise of your name. **Amen.**

The following suffrage may be omitted:

Grant that all married persons who have witnessed this exchange of vows may find their union strengthened and their loyalty confirmed. **Amen.**

Grant that the bonds of our common humanity which unite every man to his neighbour, and the living to the dead, may be transformed by your grace, that justice and peace may prevail and your will be done on earth as it is in heaven. **Amen.**

Almighty and everlasting Father, who has given to mankind the ordinance of marriage, and dost hallow it with thy blessing: bless, we beseech thee, thy servants *N* and *N*, now joined together as husband and wife; and grant that, bearing one another's burdens, sharing one another's joys, and together fulfilling the duties of their home, they may ever be faithful to each other in love and obedience to thy word; through Jesus Christ our Lord. **Amen.** (13)

Father of all mercies and giver of all grace, we commend to thee these thy servants who desire thy help and guidance for the new life which they have begun together. Grant them the grace of mutual love and forbearance; grant them thy pure and peaceable wisdom to enlighten them in all perplexities, and the power of thy spirit in their hearts to keep them constant in their trust in thee and one another. And bring them in thy goodness to thine eternal kingdom; through Jesus Christ our Lord. **Amen.** (26)

Faithful Lord, Father of love, pour down your grace upon *N* and *N*, that they may fulfil the vows they have made this day and reflect your steadfast love in their lifelong faithfulness to each other. From your great store of strength give them power and patience, affection and understanding, courage and love towards you, towards each other, and towards the world, that they may continue together in mutual growth according to your will in Jesus Christ our Lord. **Amen.**

FOR MARRIAGE IN GENERAL

Eternal God,
author of harmony and happiness,
we thank you for the gift of marriage in which men and women seek and find fulfilment, companionship, and the blessing of family life.

Give patience to those who look forward to marriage.
Give courage to those who face trials within their marriage.

Give comfort to those whose marriage has broken.
Give gratitude to those whose marriages are successful and fruitful, and let their lives reflect your love and your glory; through Jesus Christ our Lord. **Amen.** (27)

Almighty God, Father of us all,
we turn to you, the giver of all good things, and humbly thank you for all the blessings of our life.

Especially at this time we give thanks for love—for the love and concern of parents and all who have taught, guided, and cared for us through the years; and for the love and trust with which these, your children, come together now.

We thank you, too, that you have appointed marriage to guard and to strengthen and to make perfect that same gift of love.

And since we believe that it is only with your help that we can do anything well, we ask for those now before you the gift of the Holy Spirit, that in sincerity and truth they make and keep their vows; and this we ask through Jesus Christ our Lord. **Amen.**

Most holy and merciful God, by whom the solitary are set in families, we pray that your blessing may remain with *N* and *N*, now joined together in your Name. May their marriage be for them a source of great and lasting good. Spare them long to each other, and keep them faithful, tender, and true, so that they may live together in peace and holiness.

Bless them in their home and in all the works of their hands, supplying their needs and defending them from all that would harm. In prosperity may they be grateful to you, the Giver of all good: in trouble may they find that you are their refuge and their strength. So lead them through this life, we pray, that when they have fully served you in their generation, they may be received into the presence of your glory, and be numbered with those who are called to the marriage supper of the Lamb, who is Jesus Christ our Lord. **Amen.**

O gracious and merciful Father, by whose appointment marriage has been given to the human race, and by whose blessing it is strengthened and sustained, we pray for *N* and *N* now joined as husband and wife. Keep them loyal and steadfast to each other. May their love know no doubt or change, but may shared tasks, trials, and joys bind them ever more closely in heart. **Amen.**

A PRAYER FOR PARENTS AT A WEDDING

O God, whose Son Jesus Christ shared at Nazareth the life of an earthly home, we pray that he may be acknowledged as head of the household of these your children. And, as he found his authority in serving, so may they learn to serve one another in love. We remember, too, the homes from which they have come and pray that you will bless those who have given them to each other. **Amen.**

O God, by whom, in the Gospel, we are all invited to the marriage supper of your Son, so incline the hearts of these your servants that they may give obedience to your call. Bring them at the end of their days to your banqueting house, and may your banner over them be always love; through Jesus Christ our Lord. **Amen.** (28)

God, it is your work and your promise if love is found in this world. We pray that, as man and wife, as friends and neighbours, we may follow the example of your son Jesus Christ, his example of love and respect for his fellow men, so that we may in his spirit be happy and believe that you are the source of all love, that you are love itself, our God and our Father.

You who created people as man and woman, you know that it is not good for us to be alone. Renew therefore your covenant between person and person, and create a bond of affection between heart and heart. Be as close to us as the body of the other and let us experience that everything that you have made is good. **Amen.** (29)

O God, our loving heavenly Father, we thank thee for all the happiness and interest of this life, and especially for the joy of human love, by which our lives are enriched, and through which our earthly homes can give us a glimpse of the life of heaven itself. Especially at this time we thank thee for the institution of marriage, which thou hast appointed to guard, to hallow, and to perfect this sacred gift of love.

We thank thee for the love which thou hast put into the hearts of this man and this woman, and for the happiness and trust which they have found in each other. And since we can do nothing aright without thee, we pray thee to be present with us now. Help them in simple trust to commit themselves to thy loving care: may their love for each other be rooted in their love for thee, and may they enter into marriage as in thy sight and faithfully keep the vows which they are about to make; through Jesus Christ our Lord. **Amen.**

Holy Father, you created mankind in your own image
and made man and woman to be joined as husband and wife
in union of body and heart
and so fulfil their mission in this world.
Father,
to reveal the plan of your love,
you made the union of husband and wife
an image of the covenant between you and your people.
In the fulfilment of this sacrament,
the marriage of Christian man and woman
is a sign of the marriage between Christ and the Church.
Father, stretch out your hand and bless *N* and *N*. **Amen.** (30)

O God, who consecrated the state of marriage to be a sign of the spiritual unity between Christ and his Church; bless these your servants, that they may love, honour, and cherish each other in faithfulness and patience, in wisdom and true godliness, and that their home may be a haven of blessing and of peace; through Jesus Christ our Lord, who lives and reigns with you and the Holy Spirit, one God, now and for ever. **Amen.**

FOR THE GIFT OF CHILDREN

O Almighty God, Creator of mankind, who only art the well-spring of life: bestow upon these thy servants, if it be thy will, the gift and heritage of children; and grant that they may see their children brought up in thy faith and fear, to the honour and glory of thy name; through Jesus Christ our Lord. **Amen.**

We praise you, heavenly Father, for making men and women in your own image and enabling them to share in the work of your creation. Give to *N* and *N* the heritage and gift of children, and grace to bring them up in your faith and love; through Jesus Christ our Lord. **Amen.**

A PREAMBLE TO THE MARRIAGE SERVICE

We are gathered here in the presence of God to witness the marriage of *A.B.* and *C.D.* and to rejoice with them.

Marriage is a gift and calling of God and therefore it is not to be entered upon lightly or thoughtlessly, but reverently and responsibly, in obedience to the gospel of Christ.

God has provided it for the companionship of help and comfort in mutual care, so that husband and wife may live faithfully together.

God has provided it for the fulfilling of human love in mutual honour, so that husband and wife may know each other with delight.

(God has provided it for the birth and nurture of children, so that they may grow up in the security of love and the heritage of faith.)

God has provided it for the enrichment of society, so that husband and wife, being joined together, may enter into the life of the community as a new creation.

A.B. and *C.D.* now come to give their free consent and to exchange their vows of faithfulness to each other for the whole of their life together on earth.

FUNERALS

A FUNERAL SERVICE

INTRODUCTORY SENTENCES

One or more of the following sentences is said.

I am the resurrection and the life, says the Lord; he who believes in me, though he die, yet shall he live, and whoever lives and believes in me shall never die. *John 11. 25-26*

The eternal God is your dwelling place, and underneath are the everlasting arms. *Deuteronomy 33. 27*

I will never fail you nor forsake you, says the Lord. *Joshua 1. 5*

Cast your burden on the Lord, and he will sustain you. *Psalm 55. 22*

God is our refuge and strength, a very present help in trouble. *Psalm 46. 1*

In his favour is life; weeping may endure for a night, but joy comes with the morning. *Psalm 30. 5*

Blessed are those who mourn, for they shall be comforted. *Matthew 5. 4*

Blessed be the God and Father of our Lord Jesus Christ, a gentle father and the God of all consolation, who comforts us in all our sorrows, so that we offer others, in their sorrows, the consolation that we have received from God ourselves. *2 Corinthians 1. 3-4*

Blessed be the God and Father of our Lord Jesus Christ! By his great mercy we have been born anew to a living hope through the resurrection of Jesus Christ from the dead, and to an inheritance which is imperishable, undefiled, and unfading, kept in heaven for you. *1 Peter 1. 3-4*

INTRODUCTORY PRAYER

One of these prayers is used.

1 O God, Lord of life and conqueror of death, our help in every time of trouble, comfort us who mourn, and give us grace, in the presence of death, to worship you, that we may have sure hope of eternal life and be enabled to put our whole trust in your goodness and mercy; through Jesus Christ our Lord. **Amen.**

2 Eternal God our heavenly Father, who lovest us with an everlasting love, and canst turn the shadow of death into the morning; help us now to wait upon thee with reverent and submissive hearts. In the silence of this hour speak to us of eternal things, that through patience and comfort of the scriptures we may have hope, and be lifted above our darkness and distress into the light and peace of thy presence; through Jesus Christ our Lord. **Amen.**

3 Heavenly Father,
in your Son Jesus Christ
you have given us a true faith and a sure hope.
Help us to believe in the communion of saints,
the forgiveness of sins,
and the resurrection to eternal life;
through your Son Jesus Christ our Lord. **Amen.**

4 O gracious Lord, enable us to listen lovingly to your word.
May we console each other with the message you proclaim,
so finding light in darkness and faith in the midst of doubt;
through Jesus Christ our Lord. **Amen.**

THE MINISTRY OF THE WORD

One of the following Psalms may be used as a reading or said responsively.

PSALM 23

The Lord is my shepherd:
therefore can I lack nothing.
He will make me lie down in green pastures:
and lead me beside still waters.

He will refresh my soul:
and guide me in the right pathways for his name's sake.

Though I walk through the valley of the shadow of death,
  I will fear no evil:
for you are with me,
  your rod and your staff comfort me.

You spread a table before me
  in the face of those who trouble me:
you have anointed my head with oil,
  and my cup will be full.

Surely your goodness and loving-kindness
  will follow me all the days of my life:
and I shall dwell in the house of the Lord for ever. (4)

PSALM 90. 1-6, 10, 12

Lord, you have been our refuge:
from one generation to another.

Before the mountains were born
  or the earth and the world were brought to be:
from eternity to eternity you are God.

You turn man back into dust:
saying 'Return to dust, you sons of Adam.'

For a thousand years in your sight
  are like yesterday passing:
or like one watch of the night.

You cut them short like a dream:
like the fresh grass of the morning;

In the morning it is green and flourishes:
at evening it is withered and dried up.

The days of our life are three score years and ten:
or if we have strength, four score.

Teach us so to number our days:
that we may apply our hearts to wisdom. (4)

PSALM 121

I lift up my eyes to the hills:
but where shall I find help?

My help comes from the Lord:
who has made heaven and earth.

He will not suffer your foot to stumble:
and he who watches over you will not sleep.

Be sure he who has charge of Israel:
will neither slumber nor sleep.

The Lord himself is your keeper:
the Lord is your defence upon your right hand;

The sun shall not strike you by day:
nor shall the moon by night.

The Lord will defend you from all evil:
it is he who will guard your life.

The Lord will defend your going out and your coming in:
from this time forward for evermore. (4)

The following are also suitable: 39. 4-8, 12; 42. 1-7; 103. 8-18; 118. 14-21, 28-29; 130. 1-5, 7b.

One or more of the following Scripture passages is read.

Readings from the Old Testament and Apocrypha

WISDOM 4. 7-15

The virtuous man, though he die before his time, will find rest.
Length of days is not what makes age honourable,
nor number of years the true measure of life;
understanding, this is man's grey hairs,
untarnished life, this is ripe old age.
He has sought to please God, so God has loved him;
as he was living among sinners, he has been taken up.
He has been carried off so that evil may not warp his
understanding or treachery seduce his soul;
for the fascination of evil throws good things into the shade,

and the whirlwind of desire corrupts a simple heart.
Coming to perfection in so short a while, he achieved long life;
his soul being pleasing to the Lord,
he has taken him quickly from the wickedness around him.
Yet people look on, uncomprehending;
it does not enter their heads
that grace and mercy await the chosen of the Lord,
and protection, his holy ones. (7)

ISAIAH 25. 8-9; 26, 3-4

The Lord God will swallow up death for ever; he will wipe away tears from all faces, and the reproach of his people he will take away from all the earth; for the Lord has spoken. It will be said on that day, 'Lo, this is our God; we have waited for him, that he might save us. This is the Lord; we have waited for him; let us be glad and rejoice in his salvation.'

Thou dost keep him in perfect peace,
whose mind is stayed on thee,
because he trusts in thee.
Trust in the Lord for ever,
for the Lord God
is an everlasting rock. (5)

LAMENTATIONS 3. 22-26; 31-33

The steadfast love of the Lord never ceases, his compassion never fails: every morning they are renewed, so great is his faithfulness. 'The Lord is my portion', says my soul, 'therefore I will hope in him.'

The Lord is good to those who wait for him, to the soul that seeks him.

It is good to wait quietly for the salvation of the Lord. For the Lord will not cast off his servants for ever; but though he causes grief, he will have compassion in the abundance of his steadfast love; for he does not willingly afflict or punish the sons of men.

Readings from the Epistles

ROMANS 8. 18, 28, 35, 37-9

I consider that the sufferings of this present time are not worth comparing with the glory that is to be revealed to us.

We know that in everything God works for good with those who love him, who are called according to his purpose.

Who shall separate us from the love of Christ? Shall tribulation, or distress, or persecution, or famine, or nakedness, or peril, or sword?

No, in all these things we are more than conquerors through him who loved us. For I am sure that neither death, nor life, nor angels, nor principalities, nor things present, nor things to come, nor powers, nor height, nor depth, nor anything else in all creation, will be able to separate us from the love of God in Christ Jesus our Lord. (5)

ROMANS 14. 7-12

No one of us lives, and equally no one of us dies, for himself alone. If we live, we live for the Lord; and if we die, we die for the Lord. Whether therefore we live or die, we belong to the Lord. This is why Christ died and came to life again, to establish his lordship over dead and living. You, sir, why do you pass judgement on your brother? And you, sir, why do you hold your brother in contempt? We shall all stand before God's tribunal. For Scripture says, 'As I live, says the Lord, to me every knee shall bow and every tongue acknowledge God.' So, you see, each of us will have to answer for himself. (6)

1 CORINTHIANS 15. 19-23, 35-38, 42-44, 50, 53-55, 57-58

If in this life we who are in Christ have only hope, we are of all men most to be pitied. But in fact Christ has been raised from the dead, the first fruits of those who have fallen asleep. For as by a man came death, by a man has come also the resurrection of the dead. For as in Adam all die, so also in Christ shall all be made alive. But each in his own order: Christ, the first fruits, then at his coming those who belong to Christ.

But some one will ask, 'How are the dead raised? With what kind of body do they come?' You foolish man! What you sow does not come to life unless it dies. And what you sow is not the body which is to be, but a bare kernel, perhaps of wheat or of some other grain. But God gives it a body as he has chosen, and to each kind of seed its own body.

So it is with the resurrection of the dead. What is sown is perishable, what is raised is imperishable. It is sown in dishonour, it is raised in glory. It is sown in weakness, it is raised in power.

I tell you this, brethren: flesh and blood cannot inherit the kingdom of God, nor does the perishable inherit the imperishable.

For this perishable nature must put on the imperishable, and this mortal nature must put on immortality. When the perishable puts on the imperishable, and the mortal puts on immortality, then shall come to pass the saying that is written:

'Death is swallowed up in victory.
O death, where is thy victory?
O death, where is thy sting?'

But thanks be to God, who gives us the victory through our Lord Jesus Christ.

Therefore, my beloved brethren, be steadfast, immovable, always abounding in the work of the Lord, knowing that in the Lord your labour is not in vain. (5)

REVELATION 21. 1-4 and 22. 3-5

Then I saw a new heaven and a new earth; the first heaven and the first earth had disappeared now, and there was no longer any sea. I saw the holy city, and the new Jerusalem, coming down from God out of heaven, as beautiful as a bride all dressed for her husband. Then I heard a loud voice call from the throne, 'You see this city? Here God lives among men. He will make his home among them; they shall be his people, and he will be their God; his name is God-with-them. He will wipe away all tears from their eyes; there will be no more death, and no more mourning or sadness. The world of the past has gone.'

The throne of God and of the Lamb will be in its place in the city; his servants will worship him, they will see him face to face, and his name will be written on their foreheads. It will never be night again and they will not need lamplight or sunlight, because the Lord God will be shining on them. They will reign for ever and ever. (7)

2 Cor. 4. 7-18
2 Cor. 5. 1-10
These can be used as separate readings or as one reading.

1 Thess. 4. 13, 14, 18

1 Thess. 5. 1-2, 4-5, 8-11, 23

Rev. 7. 9-17

Rev. 21. 1-7

Rev. 22. 1-5

Readings from the Gospels

JOHN 6. 37-40

'All that the Father gives me will come to me; and him who comes to me I will not cast out. For I have come down from heaven, not to do my own will, but the will of him who sent me; and this is the will of him who sent me, that I should lose nothing of all that he has given me, but raise it up at the last day. For this is the will of my Father, that every one who sees the Son and believes in him should have eternal life; and I will raise him up at the last day.' (5)

JOHN 14. 1-6, 27

'Let not your hearts be troubled; believe in God, believe also in me. In my Father's house are many rooms; if it were not so, would I have told you that I go to prepare a place for you? And when I go and prepare a place for you, I will come again and will take you to myself, that where I am you may be also. And you know the way where I am going.' Thomas said to him, 'Lord, we do not know where you are going; how can we know the way?' Jesus said to him, 'I am the way, and the truth, and the life; no one comes to the Father, but by me.

Peace I leave with you; my peace I give unto you; not as the world gives do I give you. Let not your hearts be troubled, neither let them be afraid.' (5)

A sermon may be given.

Here may follow the Communion Service.

If there is no Communion a hymn may be sung, and the service proceeds as follows.

THE PRAYERS

One to be taken from each of the following groups, concluding with the Lord's Prayer.

A *Thanksgiving for the victory of Christ*

1 Praise and honour, glory and thanks be given to you, Almighty God, our Father, because in your great love for the world you gave your Son to be our Saviour, to live our life, to bear our griefs, and to die our death upon the Cross.

We praise you because you have brought him back from death with great power and glory, and given him all authority in heaven and on earth.

We thank you because he has conquered sin and death for us, and opened the kingdom of heaven to all believers.

We praise you for the great company of the faithful whom Christ has brought through death to behold your face in glory, who join with us in worship, prayer, and service.

For your full, perfect, and sufficient gift of life in Christ, all praise and thanks be given to you for ever and ever. **Amen.**

2 God of all grace, who didst send thy Son our Saviour Jesus Christ to bring life and immortality to light; we give thee thanks, that by his death he destroyed the power of death, and by his glorious resurrection opened the kingdom of heaven to all believers.

Grant us assuredly to know that because he lives we shall live also, and that neither death nor life, nor things present nor things to come, shall be able to separate us from thy love, which is in Christ Jesus our Lord. **Amen.**

We thank you, Father, that you sent your Son Jesus Christ to die for us and to rise again.

3 His cross declares your love to be without limit; his resurrection, that death, our last enemy, is overthrown.

By his victory we are assured of the promise that you will never leave us or forsake us; that neither death nor life, nor things present nor things to come, can separate us from your love, which is in Christ Jesus our Lord. **Amen.**

4 TE DEUM

You, Christ, are the King of glory:
the eternal Son of the Father.

When you became man to set us free:
you did not abhor the Virgin's womb.

You overcame the sting of death:
and opened the kingdom of heaven to all believers.

You are seated at God's right hand in glory:
We believe that you will come, and be our judge.

Come then, Lord, and help your people:
bought with the price of your own blood;

and bring us with your saints:
to glory everlasting. (3)

B *The Commendation*

Let us then entrust our *brother N* to the mercy of God our maker and redeemer.

1 O God, before whose face the generations rise and pass away, we praise thy name for all thy servants departed this life in thy faith and fear, and especially for thy servant *N*.

We thank thee for all thy goodness and loving kindness to *him* throughout the days of *his* earthly life: for all that *he* was and for all that *he* accomplished by thy grace; and that now for *him* sorrow and sickness are no more, and death is past, and that *he* lives for ever in thy love and care.

Grant that, encouraged by the example of thy saints, we may run with patience the race that is set before us, looking unto Jesus, the author and finisher of our faith, so that at the last we may be one with those we love in thy presence, where there is fullness of joy; through Jesus Christ our Lord. **Amen.**

2 All-merciful Father, we give thanks for the witness of your faithful people in all generations. Especially we give thanks for all by which *N* is remembered: for all that *he* was to those who loved *him*; and for everything in *his* life that reflected your mercy and love.

We thank you that for him sickness and sorrow are no more and that he is at rest with you.

And we pray for ourselves that, throwing off the sin which clings to us so easily, we may run with resolution the race that is set before us, looking to Jesus the pioneer and perfecter of our faith; so that, at the last, we may come, with all whom we have loved, to that abiding city where you reign, in which there is no death, no mourning and no sadness, for these have passed away; through Jesus Christ our Lord. **Amen.**

3 Heavenly Father, by thy mighty power thou gavest us life, and in thy love thou hast given us new life in Christ Jesus. We now entrust *N* to thy merciful keeping; in the faith of Jesus Christ thy Son our Lord, who died and rose again to save us, and is now alive and reigneth with thee and the Holy Spirit in glory for ever. **Amen.**

C *Prayers for those who mourn*

1 Father of mercies and God of all comfort, look in thy tender love and pity, we beseech thee, on thy sorrowing servants. Enable them to find in thee their refuge and strength, a very present help in trouble, and to know the love of Christ, which passes all understanding. Grant them faith and hope in him who by death has conquered death, and by rising again has opened the gates of everlasting life; even Jesus Christ our Lord. **Amen.**

2 God of hope and giver of all comfort, we commend to your tender care those who mourn the loss of loved ones. Give them the peace that passes all understanding, and make them to know that neither death nor life can separate them from your love in Jesus Christ our Lord. **Amen.**

3 Almighty God, Lord of life and vanquisher of death, we praise you for the sure hope of eternal life you have given us in the resurrection of our Lord Jesus Christ: and we pray that all who mourn the loss of those dear to them may enter into his victory and know his peace; for his name's sake. **Amen.**

4 Father of all mercies and God of all comfort, who madest nothing in vain, and lovest all that thou hast made: look in thy tender pity on thy bereaved servants, and enable them by thy grace to find in thee their refuge and their strength; through Jesus Christ our Lord. **Amen.**

5 Almighty God, Father of all mercies and giver of all comfort, deal graciously, we pray you, with those who mourn, that casting all their care on you they may know the consolation of your love; through Jesus Christ our Lord. **Amen.** (2)

Our Father . . .

DECLARATION OF COMMITTAL AND ENTRUSTMENT

When the whole Service takes place in a crematorium chapel the Committal follows; but if the Committal is to take place elsewhere, a hymn may be sung, and the Service ends with this sentence and a blessing.

Now may the God of peace who brought again from the dead our Lord Jesus, the great shepherd of the sheep, by the blood of the eternal covenant, equip you with everything good that you may do his will, working in you that which is pleasing in his sight, through Jesus Christ, to whom be glory for ever and ever. Amen. *Hebrews* 13. 20-21

COMMITTAL

One or more of the following sentences is said at the grave or at the crematorium.

I am the resurrection and the life, says the Lord: he who believes in me, though he die, yet shall he live, and whoever lives and believes in me shall never die. *John 11. 25-26*

Whether we live, we live to the Lord, and whether we die, we die to the Lord; so then, whether we live, or whether we die, we are the Lord's. For to this end Christ died and lived again, that he might be Lord both of the dead and of the living.
Romans 14. 8-9

Do not be afraid. I am the first and the last, says the Lord, and I am the living one; for I was dead and now I am alive for evermore, and I hold the keys of Death and Death's d omain.
Revelation 1. 17b-18a

At the grave

Having commended into the hands of God our *brother* departed, we now commit *his* body to the ground, earth to earth, ashes to ashes, dust to dust; putting our whole trust and confidence in the mercy of our heavenly Father, and in the victory of his Son, Jesus Christ our Lord, who died, was buried, and rose again for us, and is alive and reigns for ever and ever. **Amen.**

At the crematorium

Having commended into the hands of God our *brother* departed, we now commit *his* body to be cremated, ashes to ashes, dust to dust; putting our whole trust and confidence in the mercy of our heavenly Father, and in the victory of his Son, Jesus Christ our Lord, who died, was buried, and rose again for us, and is alive and reigns for ever and ever. **Amen.**

At sea

Having commended into the hands of God our *brother* departed, we now commit *his* body to the deep; putting our whole trust and confidence in the mercy of our heavenly Father, and in the victory of his Son, Jesus Christ our Lord, who died, was buried, and rose again for us, and is alive and reigns for ever and ever. **Amen.**

Then may be said:

I heard a voice from heaven, saying, 'Write this: Happy are the dead who die in the faith of Christ! Henceforth, says the Spirit, they may rest from their labours; for they take with them the record of their deeds.'

Then is said one of the following prayers.

O God, maker and redeemer of all mankind, grant to us with your servant *N* and all the faithful departed, the sure benefits of your Son's saving passion and glorious resurrection; that in the last day, when you gather up all things in Christ, we may with them enjoy the fullness of your promises; through Jesus Christ our Lord. **Amen.**

Hear, Lord, the prayers of your people, as we remember before you *N* our *brother*; and grant that we who confess your name on earth may with *him* be made perfect in the kingdom of your glory; through Jesus Christ our Lord. **Amen.**

Remember, O Lord, this servant, who has gone before us with the sign of faith, and now rests in the sleep of peace. According to your promises, grant to *him* and all who rest in Christ, refreshment, light, and peace; through Jesus Christ our Lord. **Amen.**

Father of all, by whose mercy and grace your saints remain in everlasting light and peace: we remember with thanksgiving those whom we love but see no longer; and we pray that in them your perfect will may be fulfilled; through Jesus Christ our Lord. **Amen.**

Unto him that is able to keep us from falling, and to present us faultless before the presence of his glory with exceeding joy, to the only wise God our Saviour, be glory and majesty, dominion and power, both now and for ever. **Amen.**
Jude 24, 25

THE INTERMENT OF ASHES

The service begins with a sentence from the previous services or the following:

Either

Now is Christ risen from the dead, and become the first fruits of them that slept.

or

Christ has been raised from the dead, the first fruits of those who have fallen asleep.

Having commended our *brother N* to the care of God our maker and redeemer, we now commit *his* ashes to this place, earth to earth, dust to dust; putting our whole trust and confidence in the mercy of our heavenly Father, and in the victory of his Son, Jesus Christ our Lord, who died, was buried, and rose again for us, and is alive and reigns for ever and ever. **Amen.**

Let us pray.

Either

Almighty God, grant that we, with all those who have believed in thee, may be united in the full knowledge of thy love and the unclouded vision of thy glory; through Jesus Christ our Lord. **Amen.**

or

Almighty God, grant that we, with ll those who have believed in you, may be united in the full knowledge of your love and the unclouded vision of your glory; through Jesus Christ our Lord. **Amen.**

The grace of our Lord Jesus Christ, and the love of God, and the fellowship of the Holy Spirit be with us all evermore. **Amen.**

If pastoral needs require, additional material may be used at the Committal and the Interment of the Ashes.

THE FUNERAL OF A CHILD

The Rubrics are as in the previous service.

INTRODUCTORY SENTENCES

He shall feed his flock like a shepherd. He shall gather the lambs with his arm, and carry them in his bosom. *Isaiah 40. 11*

As one whom his mother comforts, so will I comfort you, says the Lord. *Isaiah 66. 13*

Blessed are those who mourn, for they shall be comforted. *Matthew 5. 4*

I am the resurrection and the life, says the Lord; he who believes in me, though he die, yet shall he live, and whoever lives and believes in me shall never die. *John 11. 25-26*

READINGS

One of the following:

Psalm 23
2 Corinthians 1. 3-4
Matthew 18. 2-5, 10, 14
Mark 10. 13-16
Revelation 21. 4
John 14. 1-6, 18-19, 27

COMMENDATION

Almighty God, whose kingdom we cannot receive unless we be as children, we thank you for the gift of this little child. We thank you for the love and trust which *he* inspired in the hearts of those to whom *he* came: for the joy which *he* has given to all who knew *him* and for the precious memories of *him* that will abide.

Father, as your Son took little children into his arms and blessed them, take this little one into your safe keeping now and for ever.

Father in heaven, healer of broken hearts, we ask you to look in pity and compassion upon your servants whose joy has been turned into mourning. Comfort them and grant that they may be drawn closer to each other by their common sorrow. Dwell with them and be their refuge until the day break and the shadows flee away; through Jesus Christ our Lord. **Amen.**

Our Father . . . .

COMMITTAL

Jesus said:

Let the children come to me, do not hinder them; for to such belongs the Kingdom of God.

It is not the will of my Father who is in heaven that one of these little ones shall perish.

At the grave

Having commended this child *N* to the care of God our maker and redeemer, we now commit *his* body to the ground, earth to earth, ashes to ashes, dust to dust; putting our whole trust and confidence in the mercy of our heavenly Father, and in the victory of his Son, Jesus Christ our Lord, who died, was buried, and rose again for us, and is alive and reigns for ever and ever. **Amen.**

At the crematorium

Having commended this child *N* to the care of God our maker and redeemer, we now commit *his* body to be cremated, ashes to ashes, dust to dust; putting our whole trust and confidence in the mercy of our heavenly Father, and in the victory of his Son, Jesus Christ our Lord, who died, was buried, and rose again for us, and is alive and reigns for ever and ever. **Amen.**

These prayers follow.

O God, in whose mighty power it lies to bring good out of evil, and to raise up life from the dead; grant us a patient faith in time of darkness, and enlighten our understanding with the knowledge of your ways; through Jesus Christ our Lord. **Amen.**

Unto him that is able to keep us from falling, and to present us faultless before the presence of his glory with exceeding joy, to the only wise God our Saviour, be glory and majesty, dominion and power, both now and for ever. **Amen.**
Jude 24, 25

SOURCES AND ACKNOWLEDGEMENTS

1 Adapted from the Book of Common Prayer, which is Crown copyright.

2 The Prayer Book as Proposed in 1928; printed with the permission of the holders of the copyright.

3 International Consultation on English Texts; reproduced with permission.

3a International Consultation on English Texts; adapted and reproduced with permission.

4 *The Psalms: A New Translation for Worship*, © English text 1976, 1977 David L. Frost, John A. Emerton, Andrew A. Macintosh.

5 Revised Standard Version of the Bible, copyright 1946, 1952, © 1971, 1973 by the Division of Christian Education of the National Council of the Churches of Christ in the U.S.A., and used by permission.

6 New English Bible, Second Edition © 1970 by permission of Oxford and Cambridge University Presses.

7 The Jerusalem Bible, copyright © 1966 by Darton, Longman & Todd Ltd and Doubleday & Company Inc., used by permission of the publishers.

8 Translated by Robert Bridges (1844–1930); from the *Yattendon Hymnal* by permission of Oxford University Press.

9 Adapted from *New Songs for the Church*, Book 2: Canticles, published by Stainer & Bell Ltd. The words are Revised Standard Version.

11 The South African Daily Office; by permission of the Publishing Department of the Church of the Province of South Africa.

12 Ian Pitt-Watson; by permission of the author.

13 *Book of Common Worship of the Church of South India*; by permission of Oxford University Press.

13a *Book of Common Worship of the Church of South India*; adapted by permission of Oxford University Press.

13b Based on a prayer from the *Book of Common Worship of the Church of South India*; by permission of Oxford University Press.

14 Adapted from No. 556 in Frank Colquhoun, *Parish Prayers* (author unknown); by permission of Hodder & Stoughton Ltd.

15 Based on a prayer by Harold Riley in *A Book of Daily Prayer*; by permission of SPCK.

16 American Book of Common Prayer, 1928.

16a American Book of Common Prayer, 1928 (adapted).

17 Church of Scotland, Order for Holy Baptism; by permission of the Saint Andrew Press.

18 *The Unity Book of Prayer*, by the Taizé Community, translation © Geoffrey Chapman Publishers; reproduced with permission.

19 Based on a prayer from 'A Rite of Baptism for Infants', *Prayer Book Revision in Australia*, 1966; by permission of Anglican Information Office, Sydney.

20 Adapted from the Liturgy of Baptism in the English translation of the Roman Missal, © 1973 International Committee on English in the Liturgy Inc. (ICEL). All rights reserved.

22 Norman Wallwork, *A Book of Vestry Prayers*; by permission of Epworth Press.

23 Church of England Liturgical Commission, unpublished text; reproduced with permission.

24 *Prayer Book Studies 24: Pastoral Offices*, © Copyright 1970 by Charles Mortimer Guilbert as Custodian of the Standard Book of Common Prayer. All rights reserved. Reprinted by permission.

25 Alternative Services Series 3, The Marriage Service, © The Registrars of the Provinces of Canterbury and York 1975, 1976.

26 *A Form of Prayer for use in church after a civil marriage* (Salisbury, England); by permission of the Bishop of Salisbury.

27 Michael Saward, *Task Unfinished*; by permission of Falcon Books.

28 *Worship Now*, published by the Saint Andrew Press, Edinburgh, 1972; reproduced with permission.

29 Huub Oosterhuis, *Your Word Is Near*, copyright © 1968 by The Missionary Society of St Paul the Apostle in the State of New York, slightly adapted; by permission of Paulist Press.

30 English translation of the Rite of Marriage, © 1970 International Consultation on English in the Liturgy (ICEL). All rights reserved.

31 *Apostolic Constitutions*, adapted.

Apart from the use of the Revised Standard Version of the Bible acknowledged under 5 above, most biblical passages not identified as a particular translation are based on this version.